• Barth

EDINBURGH
Streetfinder
COLOUR STREET ATLAS

C000051271

CONTENTS

Legend	2
Key to Map Pages	4
City Centre Map	6
Map Pages	8
Route Planning Maps	52
Index	56

Bartholomew
A Division of HarperCollins*Publishers*

Legend / Légende / Zeichenerklärung

Legend to main map section, pages 8-51.

main through road
axe principal
Durchgangsstraße

dual carriageway
chaussées séparées
Straße mit getrennten Fahrbahnen

main link road
axe secondaire
Verbindungsstraße

other roads
autres rues
sonstige Straßen

lane, drive
petite rue, allée
Gasse, Einfahrt

walkway
passage
Fußgängerweg

path
sentier
Pfad

shopping centre
centre commerçant
Einkaufszentrum

tourist information centre
syndicat d'initiative
Informationsbüro

car park
parking / Parkplatz

taxi rank
station de taxi / Taxistand

toilets
toilettes / Toiletten

post office
bureau de poste / Postamt

George **principal hotel**
hôtel important / führendes Hotel

consulate *
consulat / Konsulat

public building
bâtiment public / öffentliches Gebäude

church
église / Kirche

tower block
immeuble élevé / Hochhaus

King's **theatre**
théâtre / Theater

Cannon **cinema**
cinéma / Kino

Usher Hall **public hall**
salle de réunion / Veranstaltungshalle

Tolbooth **museum or gallery**
musée ou galerie d'art / Museum

library
bibliothèque / Bibliothek

primary school
école primaire / Grundschule

secondary school
école secondaire / Höhere Schule

hospital
hôpital / Krankenhaus

police station
poste de police / Polizeiwache

fire station
pompiers / Feuerwache

railways
lignes ferroviaires
Eisenbahnlinien

main station
gare principale
Hauptbahnhof

airport coach terminal
aérogare
Abfahrt zum Flughafen

bus route
ligne d'autobus
Omnibusroute

5 C1 **bus terminus** / *terminus d'autobus*
Omnibusendhaltestelle L.R.T. / E.Sc.

one-way street
sens unique / Einbahnstraße

traffic lights
feu de signalisation / Verkehrsampel

dense built-up area
noyau urbain
dicht bebautes Gebiet

open residential area
zone résidentielle
dünn bebaute Wohnfläche

industrial land
terrain industriel
Industriegelände

open land
terrain non loti
unbebautes Gebiet

park
jardin / Park

woodland
terrain boisé / Wald

picturesque road / *route pittoresque*
landschaftlich schöne Straße

viewpoint
point de vue / Aussichtspubkt

cemetery
cimetière / Friedhof

recreation area
terrain de sport / Sportgelände

golf course
golf / Golfplatz

B   **bowling green**
boules / Bowlingplatz

T   **tennis court**
tennis / Tennisplatz

swimming pool
piscine / Schwimmbad

sailing centre
centre de voile / Segelhafen

caravan / camping site
caravaning / camping / Campingplatz

EH 5   **postal boundary**
limite de district postal
Postbezirksgrenze

* For consulate abbreviation see index

Scale of main map pages - 1:15 000 (4.2 inches to 1 mile)

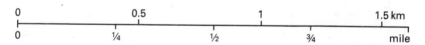

0	0.5	1	1.5 km
0	¼	½	¾	mile

© Bartholomew 1991
Bartholomew is a Division of HarperCollins Publishers

ISBN 0 7028 2076 8

Printed by Bartholomew, HarperCollins Manufacturing,
in Edinburgh, Scotland.

D/B 4298 UNC

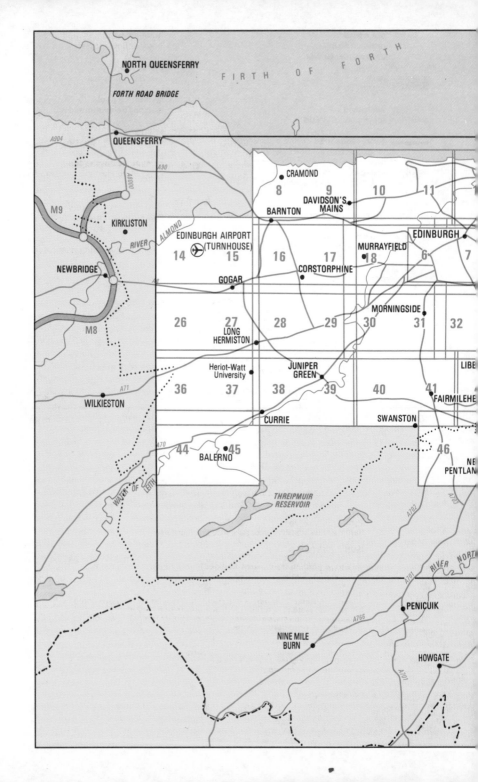

KEY TO MAP PAGES

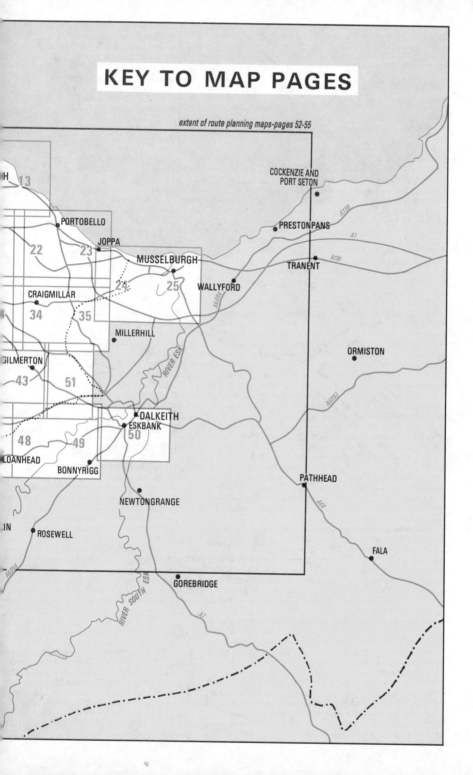

extent of route planning maps-pages 52-55

COCKENZIE AND
PORT SETON

H 13

PORTOBELLO

JOPPA

22 23

MUSSELBURGH

24 25 WALLYFORD

CRAIGMILLAR

34 35

MILLERHILL

PRESTONPANS

A198

A1

TRANENT

A199

A6094

RIVER ESK

ORMISTON

GILMERTON

43 51

A6093

DALKEITH
ESKBANK
50

48 49

LOANHEAD

BONNYRIGG

NEWTONGRANGE

PATHHEAD

A68

LIN

ROSEWELL

A6094

RIVER SOUTH ESK

GOREBRIDGE

A7

FALA

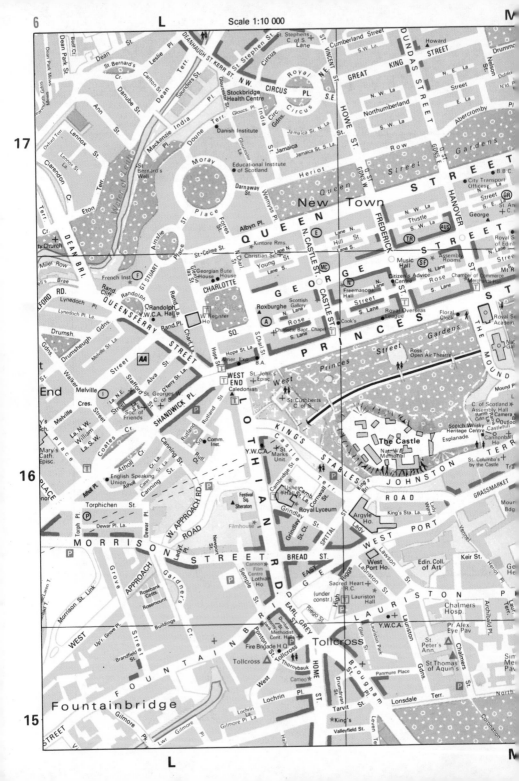

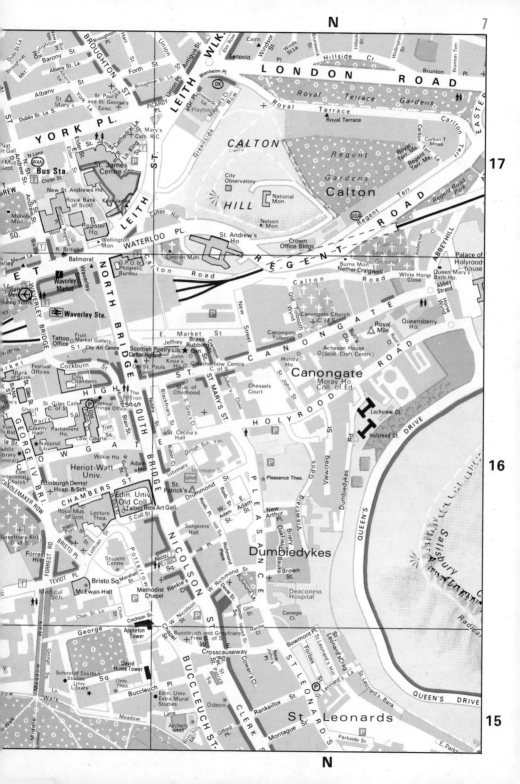

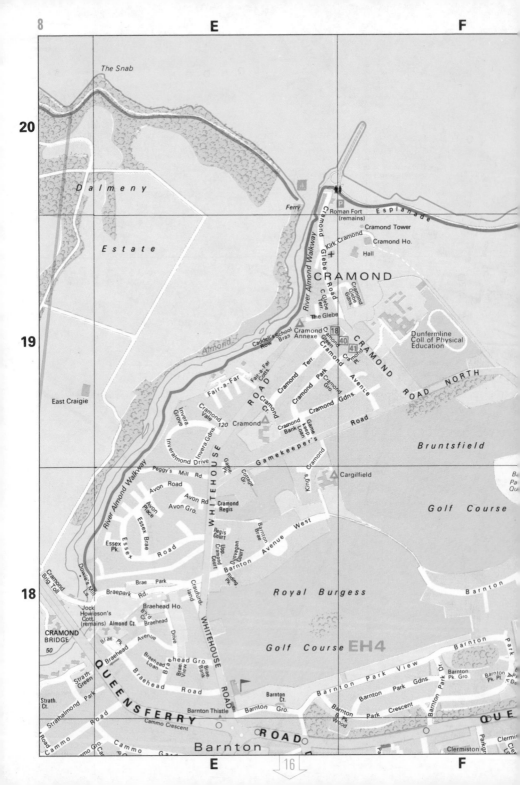

20

The Snab

Dalmeny

Estate

Ferry

Cramond Glebe Road

River Almond Walkway

Roman Fort
(remains)

Esplanade

Cramond Tower

Kirk Cramond

Cramond Ho.

Hall

CRAMOND

Cramond
Glebe
Gdns.

The Glebe

19

East Craigie

Almond

Caddell's Row

Cramond
Annexe

School
Brae

Cramond Green

18
40
41

Cramond Pl.

CRAMOND ROAD NORTH

Dunfermline
Coll. of Physical
Education

Fair-a-Far

Fair-a-Far Cotts.

Cramond Terr.

Cramond Park

Cramond Avenue

Cramond Gdns.

Cramond Road

Invera Grove

Cramond Vale

Invera Gdns.

120 Cramond

Cramond Bank

Game Keep

King's Cramond

Gamekeeper's

Bruntsfield

Inveralmond Drive

Game Gr.

Cottage Gr.

Cargilfield

Peggy's Mill Rd.

Avon Road

Avon Rd.

Whitehouse Road

Cramond Regis

King's Cramond

Golf Course

Avon Place

Avon Gro.

Essex Brae

Essex Road

Regis Court

Upp Cramond Court

Dunnegan Court

Barnton Road

Barnton Brae

Avenue West

Royal Burgess

Essex Pk.

Essex

Dowie's Mill

River Almond Walkway

Cramond Brig Toll

Brae Park

Braepark Rd.

Craufurdland

Whitehouse Road

Golf Course

EH4

Barnton

CRAMOND
BRIDGE

50

Jock Howieson's Cott. (remains)

Almond Ct.

Braehead Ho.

Braehead

Blae Pk.

Braehead Avenue

Braehead Drive

Braehead Gro.

Braehead View

Braehead Bank

Braehead Loan

Braehead Road

Strath Green

Strath. Ct.

Strahalmond Park

QUEENSFERRY

Road

Cammo

Cammo Gro.

Cammo Crescent

Barnton Ct.

Barnton Gro.

Barnton Thistle

Barnton Park View

Barnton Park Gdns.

Barnton Park Crescent

Barnton Wood

Barnton Park Dr.

Barnton Pk. Gro.

Barnton Pk. Pl.

Barnton Park

ROAD

Barnton

Clermiston

QUE

18

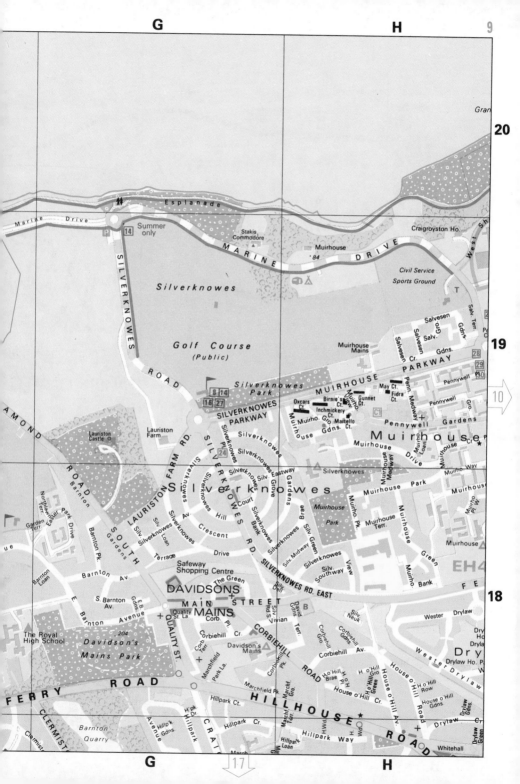

Gran

E s p l a n a d e

M a r i n e   D r i v e

Summer only

P   14

Stakis Commodore

Craigroyston Ho.

M A R I N E   D R I V E

Muirhouse 84

West Sh

Civil Service Sports Ground

T

Salv. Terr

Silverknowes

Muirhouse Mains

Salvesen
Salvesen
Salv. Gro
Salv.
Cr.
Salvesen Gdns.

S I L V E R K N O W E S   R O A D

Golf Course
(Public)

Muirhouse Mains

Pennywell Gro

28
29
P10

Pennywell

Silverknowes Park

M U I R H O U S E   P A R K W A Y

Penn Medway

May Ct.
Fidra Ct.

Pennywell
Gro

8 14
16 27

Oxcars
Birnie's
Inchmickery
Gunnet Ct.
Muirho.
Ct.
Maltello
Ct.

Muirho.

Pennywell Gardens

S I L V E R K N O W E S   P A R K W A Y

Muirho. Gro
Muiro. Gdns.

C1

Muirhouse Cr.

Lauriston Castle

Lauriston Farm

Muirhouse

Muirhouse Loan

Muirhouse Drive

Silverknowes

Silverknowes

Muirho. Way

Muirho. Way

EH4

D I A M O N D   R O A D

Garden Terr.
Northlawn Terr.

L A U R I S T O N   F A R M   R D.

S I L V E R K N O W E S   H I L L

Silverknowes Bank

Silverknowes Eastway

Silverknowes Grove

Silverknowes

Silverknowes

Muirhouse Park

Muirho. Pk.

Muirhouse Terr.

Muirhouse Green

Muirhouse

Barnton Park Drive

Park Pk.

Silv. Gardens

Silv. Loan

S O U T H

Silverknowes Avenue

Silverknowes Terrace

Silverknowes Court

Silverknowes Crescent

Silverknowes Drive

Silverknowes Bank

Silverknowes Brae

Silv. Green

Silv. Midway

Silverknowes

Silv. Southway

Silv. View

Muirho. Bank

F E

Barnton Loan

Barnton Pk.

S. Barnton Av.

Barnton Av.

E.B. Gdns.

The Green

Safeway Shopping Centre

S I L V E R K N O W E S   R D.   E A S T

David Gdns

Silv. Rd's Way

B

Silv Neuk

Wester Drylaw

Drylaw

Dry
Ho
Dryla

DAVIDSONS

M A I N   S T R E E T

MAINS

Quality St. La.

Corb. Pl.

David Terr.

St. Vivian

Corbiehill Gro

Corbiehill Gdns

Corbiehill Av.

Wester Drylaw

Drylaw Ho. P.

Dry

The Royal High School

204

Davidson's Mains Park

Q U A L I T Y   S T.

Corb. Terr

Corbiehill Cr.

Marchfield Park La.

Davidson's Mains

C O R B I E H I L L   R O A D

Corbiehill Pk.

Ho'Hill Brae

Ho. o'Hill Gro
Ho.o'Hill Green

H. o'Hill Row

House o'Hill Cr.

House o'Hill Gdns.

W e s t e r D r y l a w

House o'Hill Road

D r y

Drylaw Gdns.

F E R R Y   R O A D

Barnton Quarry

H'pk. Dr.

Hillpk Gdns

Hillpark

H I L L H O U S E

Marchfield Pk.

Marchf. Terr

Hillpark Ct.

Hillpark Cr.

Hillpark Way

Hillpark Loan

Marchf.
Gro.

R O A D

House o'Hill Av.

Whitehall

Drylaw Green

Dryla

C L E R M I S T

C R A I

Marsh

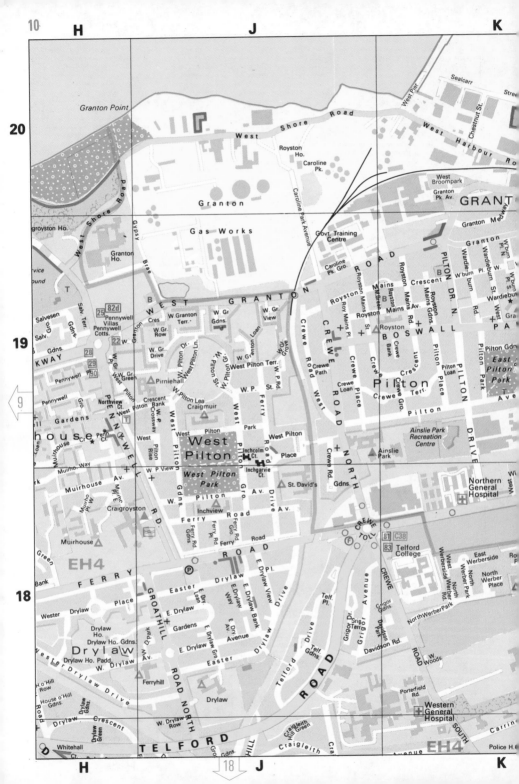

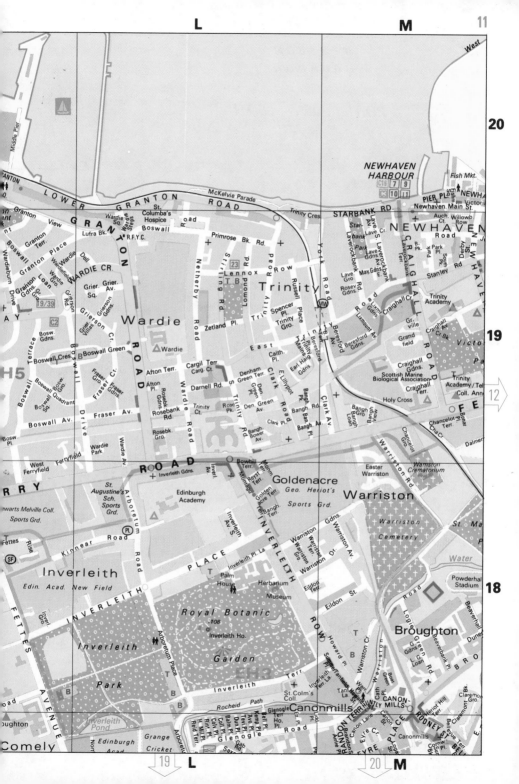

EDINBURGH

DOCK

MARINE Rd

Bath Rd.

Albert Rd.

Carron Pl.

AMANDER STREET

Marine

Esplanade

Links Gdns.

△ St. Mary's

Links

B

Seafield Pl.

SEAFIELD ROAD

Sewage Works

Seafield

CLAREMONT PARK

Gladstone Pl.

Summer. Gdns.

Claremt. Gdns.

Blackie Rd.

Claremt. Clarebk.

Pirniefield Terr.

Pirniefield Bank

Pirniefield Terr. Rd.

Boothacre La.

Seafield Gdns.

Seafield Av.

Searcot

Pirniefield Bank

Seafield Cemetery & Crematorium

Seal St.

Pirniefield Place

Prospect Bank Rd.

Prospect Bank

Prospect Bank Terr.

P. Bank Pl.

Prospect Bank Gro.

Ryehill Terr.

Rye Terr.

Rye Gro.

RESTALRIG

Rye Av.

Ryehill Gro.

P. Bank Gdns.

Bank Pl.

✠ Eastern General Hospital

Restalrig

Craigentinny Av. North

Seafield Recreation Ground

57

Seafield Way

FILLYSIDE RD.

Seafield Way

18

Hawkhill Ct.

Restalrig Pk.

Nisbet Ct. Av.

Restalrig ROAD

Circus

Restalrig Ct.

Restalrig Square

Findlay Cotts.

Findlay Medway

Findlay Gdns.

Findlay Gro.

Findlay Avenue

Craigentinny Golf Course

Nantwich Dr.

AVENUE

Fillyside Terr.

Fillyside Av.

Seafield Drive

Cat & Dog Home

SEAF

Lochend

SLEIGH

Lochend

Lochend

DRIVE

34 36

Sleigh Gdns.

87

RESTALRIG

C13

CRAI

(Public)

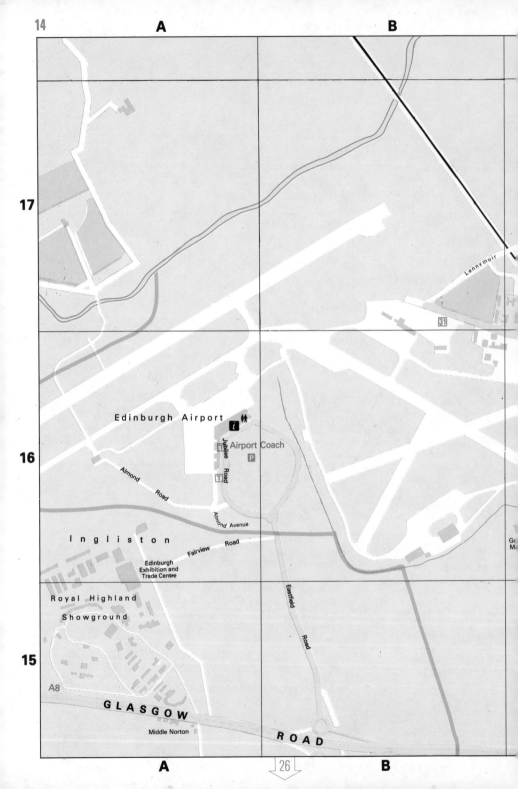

A B

Lennymuir

31

Edinburgh Airport

i ♁

T Jublee

Airport Coach

P

Almond Road

T

Jublee Road

Almond Avenue

I n g l i s t o n

Fairview Road

Edinburgh
Exhibition and
Trade Centre

Eastfield Road

Go
Ma

Royal Highland

Showground

A8

G L A S G O W

R O A D

Middle Norton

A B

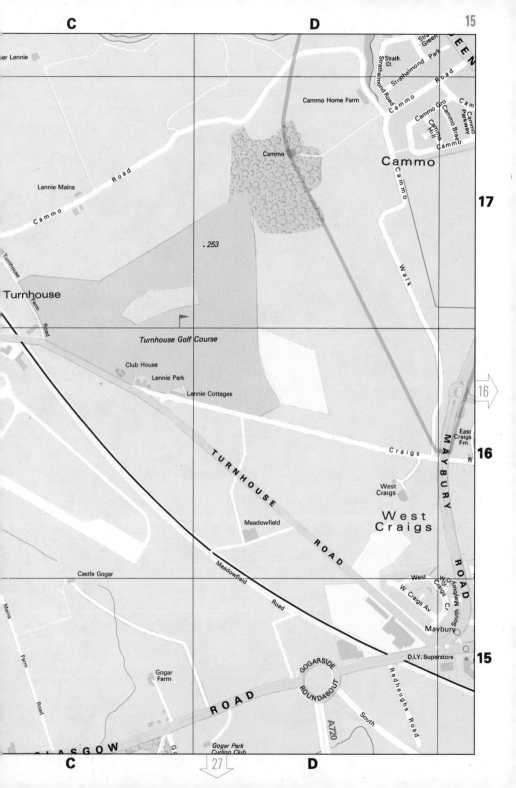

er Lennie

Strath. Green
Strath. Ct.
Strathalmond Park
Cammo Home Farm
Strathalmond Road
C a m m o
Road
Cammo Gro.
Cammo Hill
Cammo Braehead
Cammo Parkway
C a m m o
Cammo

Cammo

Lennie Mains

Road

C a m m o

. 253

C a m m o

W a l k

Turnhouse

Turnhouse Farm
Road

Turnhouse Golf Course

Club House
Lennie Park
Lennie Cottages

T U R N H O U S E

C r a i g s

M A Y B U R Y

East Craigs Fm.
R

West Craigs

West Craigs

R O A D

Meadowfield

Castle Gogar

Meadowfield
Road

West Craigs
W. Cr.
W.Cr. Cr.
Kingsknowe
R O A D

Maybury

Mains
Farm

Gogar Farm

GOGARSIDE
ROUNDABOUT

D.I.Y. Superstore

Redheughs Road

West

W. Craigs Av.

G L A S G O W
R O A D

A720

South

Gogar Park
Curling Club

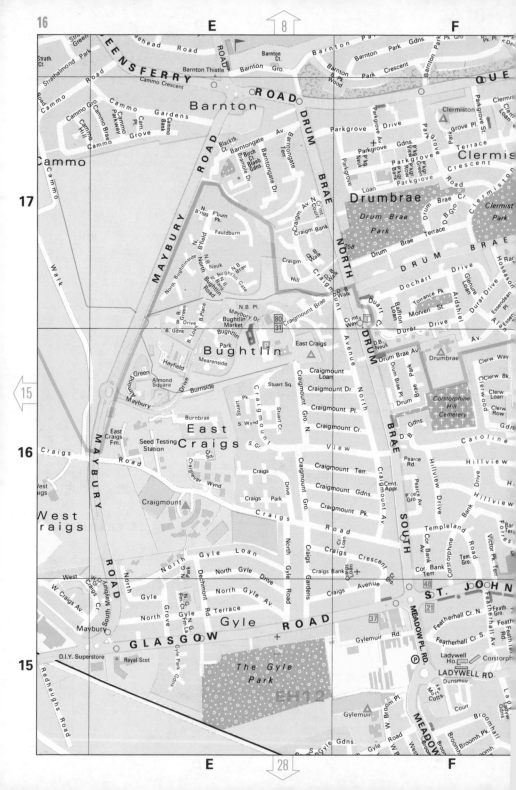

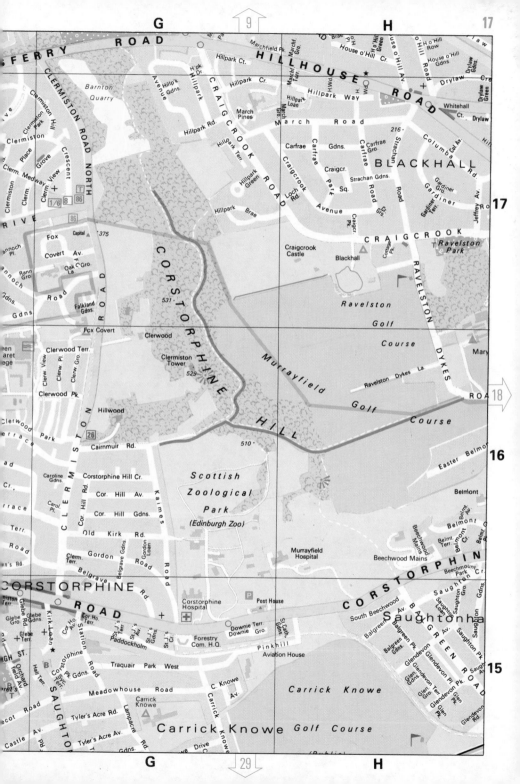

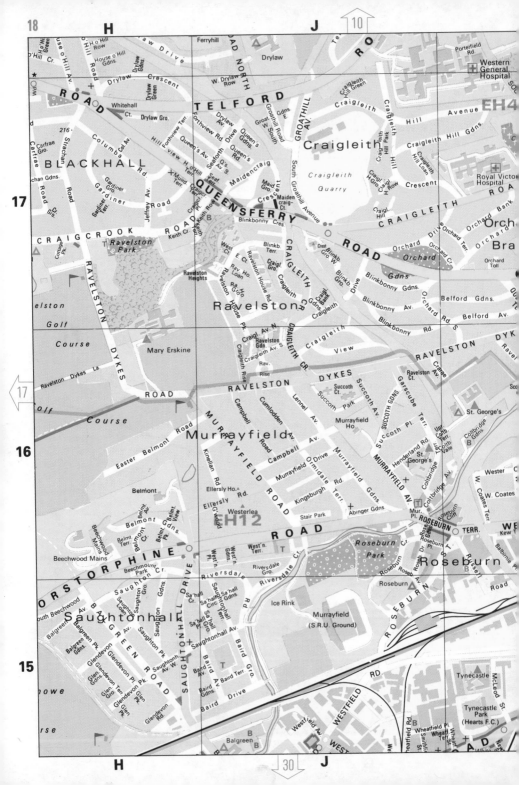

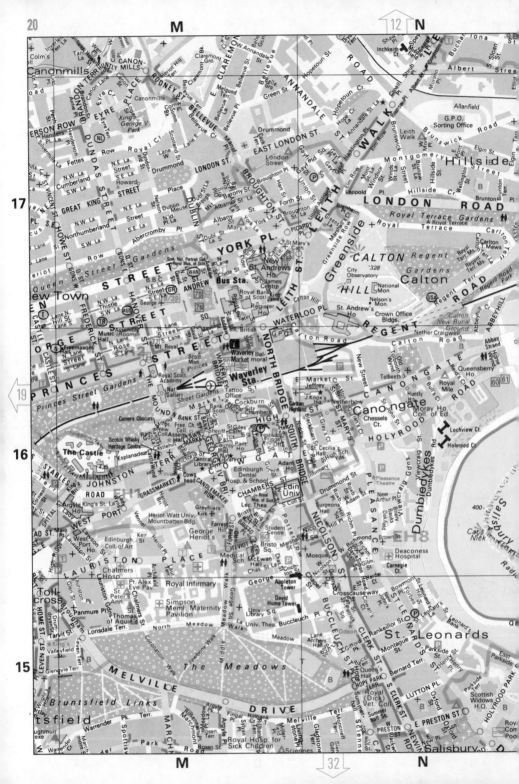

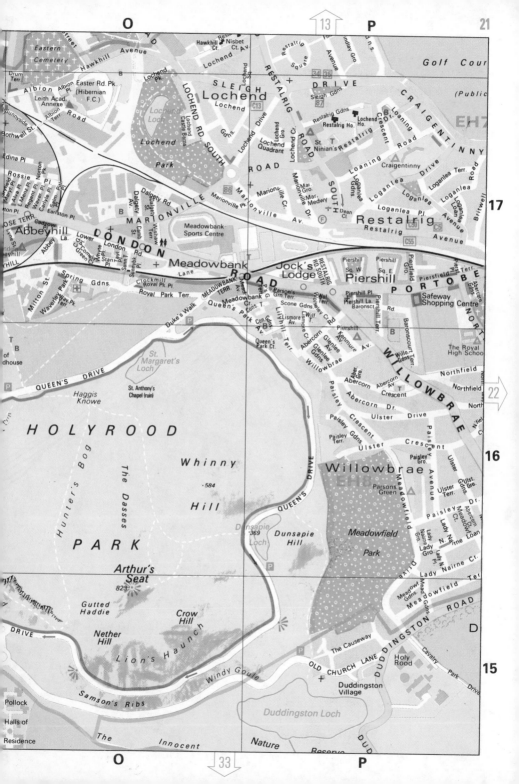

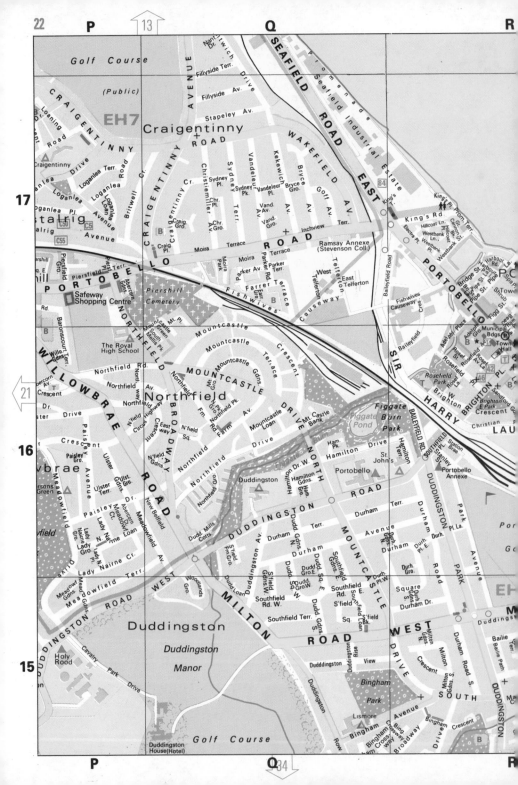

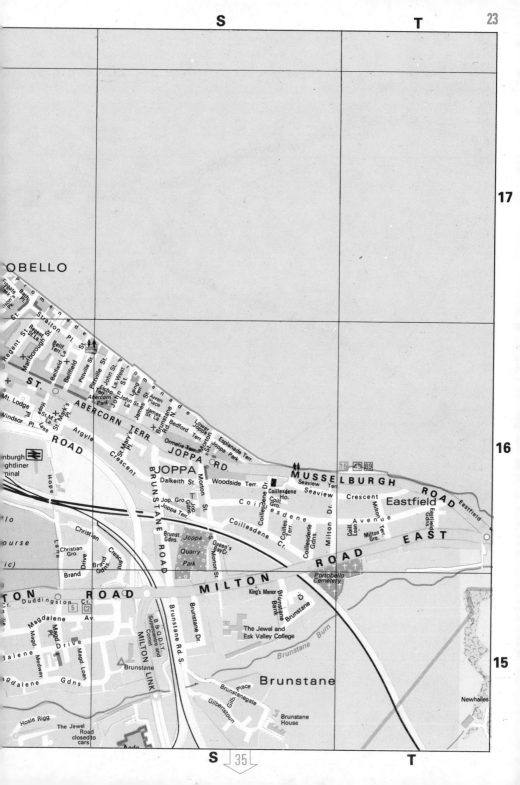

16

15

OBELLO

Promenade

Figgate Bank

Fishers Bay

St.

Straiton Pl.

Regent St.
St. La.
Marlborough

Bellf.
Terr. La.

Bellfield

Bellfield

Pitville St.

Pitville St.

Abercorn
Park

John St.
John St. La.

Elcho
Terr.

La. West
Joppa

St. Mary's

James
St.

St. Areen
Place

Lower
Joppa

Brunstane
Rd.

Bedford Terr.

Morton
St.

Ormelie Terr.

Esplanade Terr.

Joppa Park

PROMENADE

ST.

ABERCORN TERR.

Mt. Lodge

St. Mark's

St. Mark's Pl.

Windsor Pl.

ROAD

Argyle

Crescent

Hope

Lane

burgh
Lightliner
minal

Edinburgh
Lightliner
Terminal

JOPPA RD.

JOPPA

BRUNSTANE ROAD

Dalkeith St.

Jop. Gro.
Gdns.

Joppa Terr.

Morton
St.

Woodside Terr.

Coillesdene Dr.

Coillesdene

Coilles
dene Cr.

Coillesdene
Gdns.

Coilles.
Terr.

Coill.
Gro.

MUSSELBURGH

Seaview
Terr.

Seaview

Crescent

ROAD

Eastfield

Eastfield

15 45 89

Milton Dr.

Avenue

Coill.
Loan

Milton Terr.

Milton
Gro.

Eastfield
Gdns.

Christian

Christian
Gro.

Brand
Gdns.

Crescent

Drive

Brunst.
Gdns.

Joppa
Quarry
Park

Queen's
Bay Cr.

Morton St.

ourse

(ic)

Brand

MILTON

ROAD

EAST

King's Manor

Portobello
Cemetery

Brunstane
Bank

Brunstane

Duddingston

Cr.

5

C2

Av.

Magdalene

Magd.
Pl.

Magd.
Loan

Drive

alene

Medway

Magdalene
Gdns.

Magd

dalene

Hosie Rigg

The Jewel
Road
closed to
cars

Ayde

MILTON

ROAD

MILTON LINK

B & Q D.I.Y.
Supercentre and
Comet

Brunstane Dr.

Brunstane Rd. S.

Brunstane

The Jewel and
Esk Valley College

Brunstanegate

Brunstane
Place

Gibb

Gilberstoun

Brunstane
House

Brunstane

Brunstane Burn

Newhailes

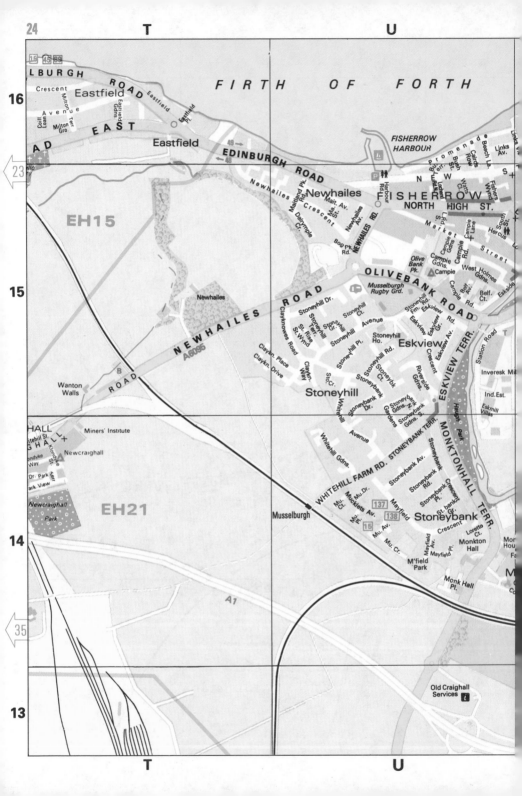

T   U

16

LBURGH   ROAD

Crescent   Eastfield

Avenue

Coill Loan   Milton Ter.

Milton Gro.

Eastfield Gdns.

Eastfield Pl.

EAST

Eastfield

AD

23

EH15

EDINBURGH ROAD

FIRTH   OF   FORTH

FISHERROW HARBOUR

Eastfield

49 →
← 48

Newhailes Crescent

Maitland Pk.

Mait. Av.

Newhailes

Dalrymple Ct.

Bog Pk. Rd.

NEWHAILES RD.

Promenade

Beach La.
Cairns Row

Links Av.

Harbour Rd.

FISHERROW

NORTH   HIGH ST.

N   W

Watts Wynd

Bush St.

Fishers Wynd

South St.

Hercus

Market   Street

Campie Gdns.

Campie Rd.

Temple Lane

West Holmes Gdns.

Eskside

Belf. Ct.

15

Newhailes

NEWHAILES   ROAD

A6095

Claykn. Place

Claykn. Drive

Clayknowes Road

OLIVEBANK ROAD

Olive Bank Pk.

Campie Gdns.

Campie

Musselburgh Rugby Grd.

Stoneyhill Dr.

Stoneyhill Ct.

Stoneyhill Terr.

St. Wynd

St. Rise

Stoneyhill Pl.

Stoneyhill Av.

Avenue

Stoneyhill Rd.

Stoneyhill Ho.

Eskview

Station Road

Inveresk Mil

Ind. Est.

Eskmill Villas

Eskview Rd.

Eskview Gr.

Eskview Av.

Crescent

Olive Bank Rd.

Campie Lm.

ESKVIEW TERR.

Haugh Park

B

ROAD

Wanton Walls

Stoc.Cr.

Clayk. Way

Stoneyhill Ct.

Stoneyhill Gr.

Riverside Gdns.

Stoneyhill

Stoneyhill Pl.

Stoneybank

Stoneybank Gdns.

Stoneybank Gdns. Z

Stoneybank Gdns. S

Whitehill

Stoneybank Dr.

MONKTONHALL TERR.

14

HALL

GHALL

Whitehill St.

Kirrof St.

ondyke Way

Dr. Park

ark View

Miners' Institute

Newcraighall

EH21

Newcraighall Park

Whitehill Gdns.

Avenue

WHITEHILL FARM RD.

STONEYBANK TERR.

Musselburgh

Mu. Ct.

Mu.Dr.

Mucklets Av.

Mu. Pl.

137

138

16

Mayfield

Stoneybank Av.

Stoneybank Rd.

Stoneybank Pl.

Stoneybank Cres.

St. banks Gr.

Stoneybank

Crescent

Loretta Ct.

Monkton Hall

Mor Hou Fa

35

A1

M'field Park

Mu. Av.

Mu. Cr.

Mayfield Av.

Mayfield Pl.

Stoneybank

Monk Hall Pl.

M

13

Old Craighall Services

T   U

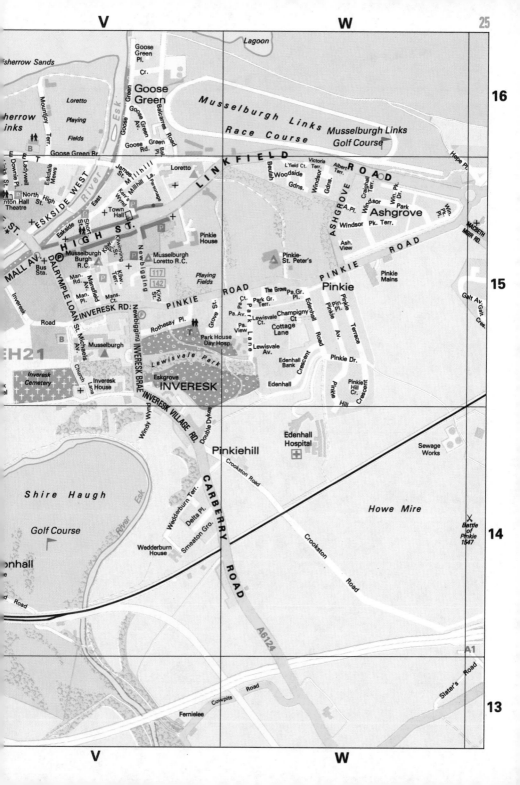

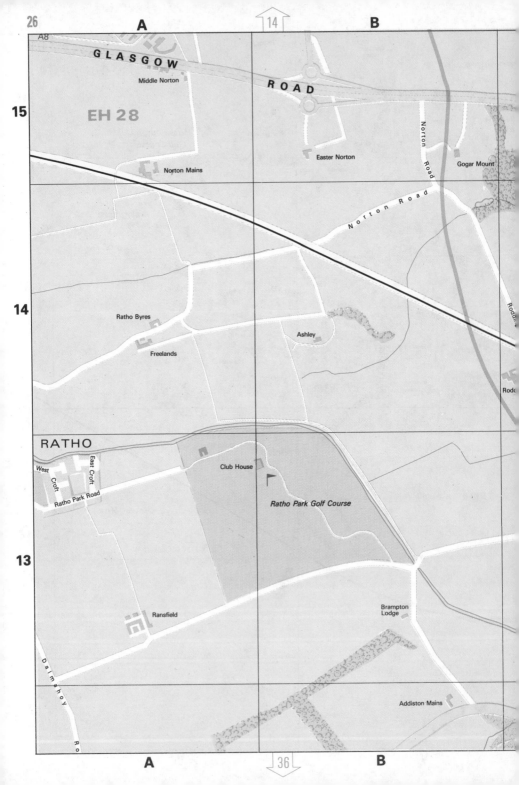

A

B

A8

GLASGOW

Middle Norton

ROAD

15

EH 28

Easter Norton

Norton Road

Gogar Mount

Norton Mains

Norton Road

Rodd

14

Ratho Byres

Ashley

Freelands

Rodd

RATHO

West Croft

East Croft

Club House

Ratho Park Road

Ratho Park Golf Course

13

Ransfield

Brampton Lodge

Dalmahoy Ro

Addiston Mains

A

B

Road

G L A S G O W   R O A D

ROUNDABOUT

A720

South

heughs Road

Gyle

Gogar Park
Curling Club

Gogar

Gogarburn Hospital

Station

T H E   C I T Y   O F   E D I N B U R G H   B Y P A S S

Road

Millburn Tower

Redheughs

Gogar
Green

Kellerstane

Gogarburn
Farm

Gogar

Burn

Gogarbank

Gogar

Station

Road

Over Gogar

Trefoil School

Hermiston House Road

Long
Hermiston

Union Canal

Hermiston
House

West
Hermiston

Mid Hermiston

RICCARTON

C A L D E R   R O A D

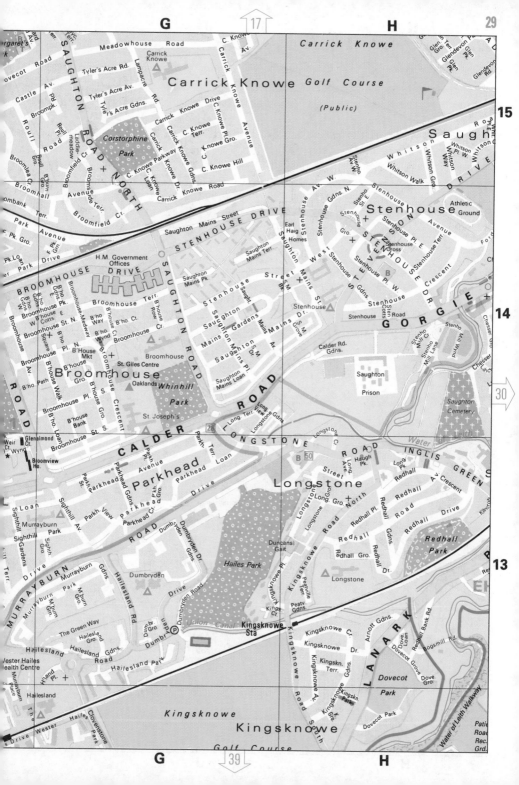

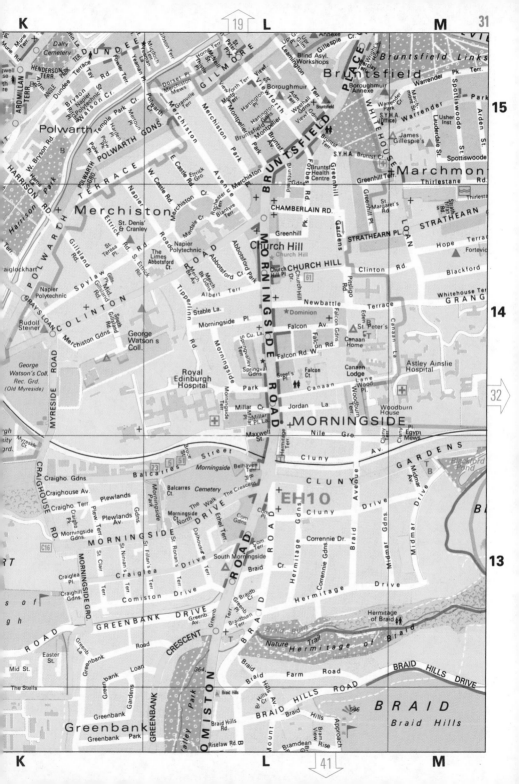

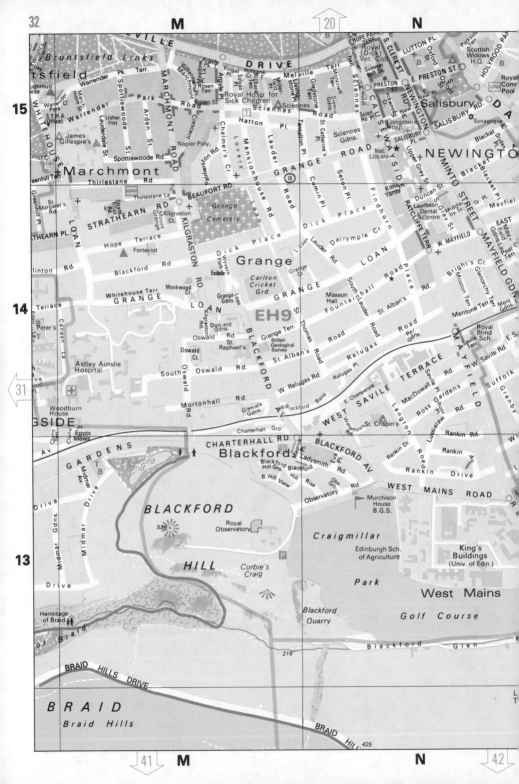

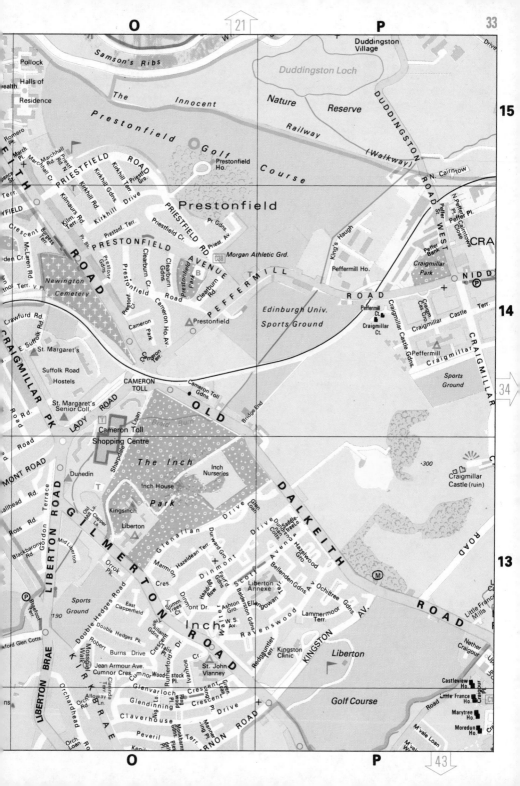

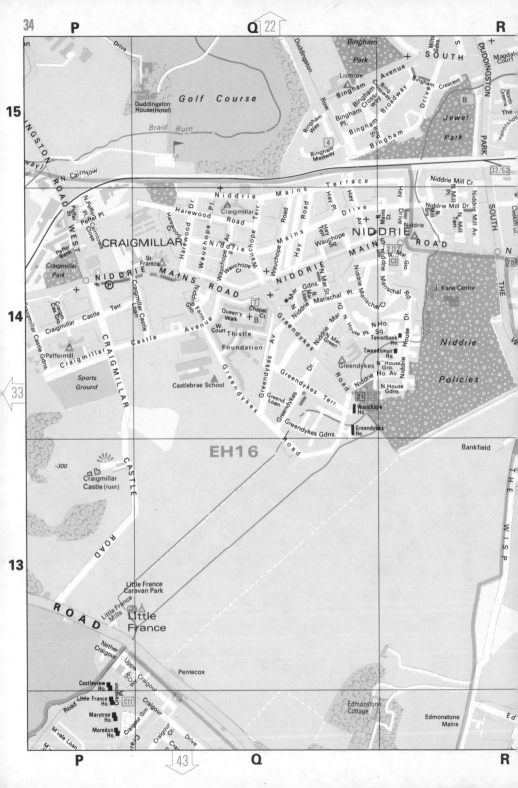

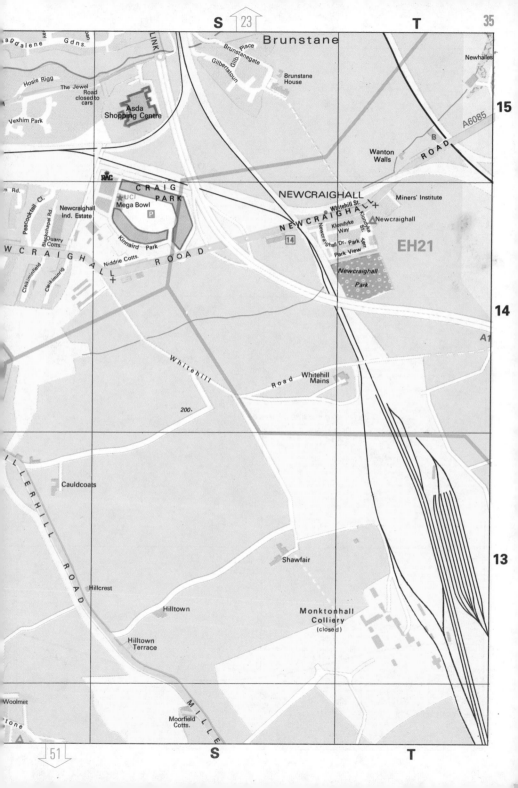

Brunstane

Newhailes

Magdalene Gdns.

Hosie Rigg

The Jewel
Road
closed to
cars

Vexhim Park

Asda
Shopping Centre

LINK

Brunstanegate
Gilb Place
Gilbertstoun

Brunstane
House

Wanton
Walls

ROAD
A6085

B

15

RAC

CRAIG PARK

UCI
Mega Bowl
P

Newcraighall
Ind. Estate

n Rd.

Peacocktail Ct.
Blackchapel Rd.
Quarry Cotts.

Kinnaird Park

Niddrie Cotts.

WCRAIGHALL

Chalkimfield
Chalkimrig

NEWCRAIGHALL

NEWCRAIGHALL

Miners' Institute

Whitehill St.
Newcraighall Dr.
Klondyke Way
Park View

Klondyke St.
Park Kerr
Newcraighall

EH21

Newcraighall
Park

ROAD

14

Whitehill

Road
Whitehill
Mains

200

A1

14

ILLERHILL ROAD

Cauldcoats

Hillcrest

Hilltown

Hilltown
Terrace

Shawfair

Monktonhall
Colliery
(closed)

13

Woolmet

stone

Moorfield
Cotts.

MILLE

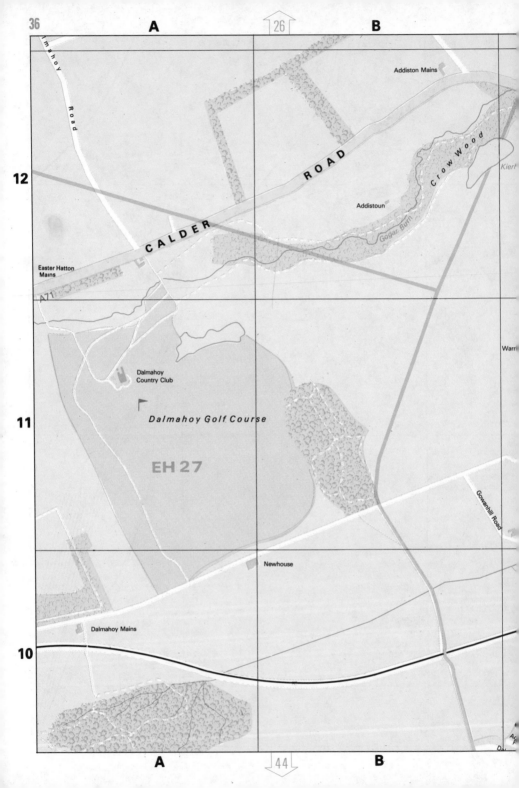

Addiston Mains

Crow Wood

Kier

R O A D

12

C A L D E R

Addistoun

Gogar Burn

Easter Hatton
Mains

A71

Warri

Dalmahoy
Country Club

11

Dalmahoy Golf Course

EH 27

Gowanhill Road

Newhouse

Dalmahoy Mains

10

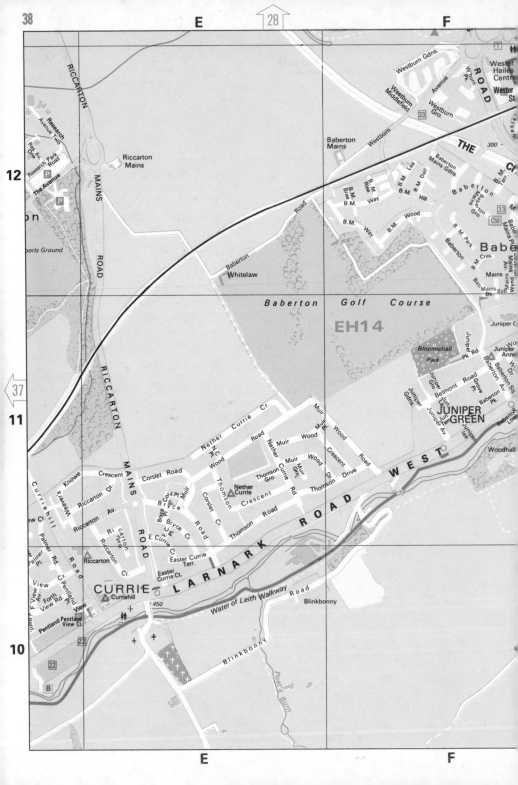

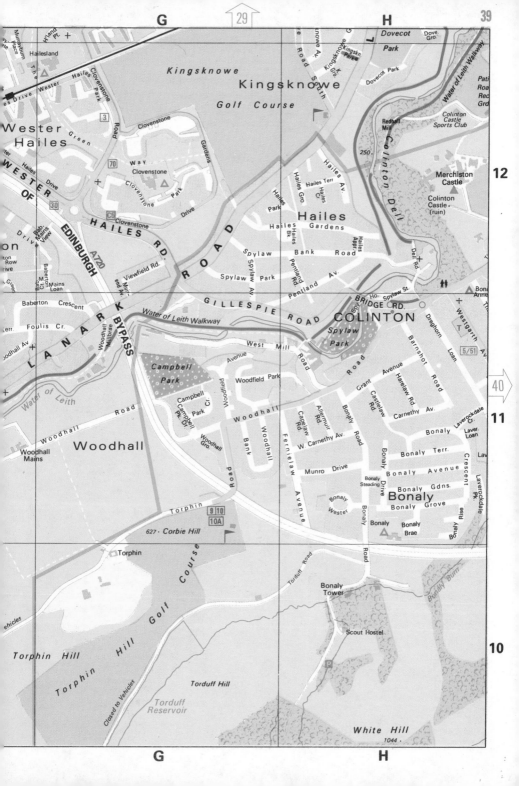

Murrayburn
H'land Pt.
Hailesland
Murrayburn
Place

Wester Hailes Park
Clovenstone

Kingsknowe
Kingsknowe
Kingsknowe
Golf Course

Dovecot
Park
Dove
Gro.

Water of Leith Walkway

Pati
Roa
Rec
Grd

Redhall
Mill

Colinton
Castle
Sports Club

**Wester
Hailes**

Clovenstone
Road
Way
Clovenstone

Green

3

70

Clovenstone
Park
Clovenstone
Drive
Gardens

Hailes Av.
Hailes Gro.
Hailes Terr.
Hailes Cr.

250.

Colinton Dell

Merchiston
Castle

**WESTER
OF
EDINBURGH**

A720
HAILES RD.
30
C6

Viewfield Rd.
Mains View
Baberton
Mains Loan

Hailes
Park
Hailes
Bk.

ROAD

Hailes Gro.
Hailes
Bank
Spylaw
Road

Hailes
Gardens
Hailes
Appr.

Colinton
Castle
(ruin)

Dell Rd.

Baberton Crescent

Spylaw
Spylaw Park
Spylaw Av.

Pentland Rd.
Pentland Av.

Bona
Anne

12

Foulis Cr.

Water of Leith Walkway
Millbrae
Woodhall

GILLESPIE ROAD

BRIDGE RD.
Spylaw Ho.
Spylaw St.

COLINTON

Dreghorn

Westgarth Av.

T

5/51

LANARK BYPASS

Campbell
Park

Avenue
Woodfield Park

West Mill
Road

Spylaw
Park

Barnshot Road

Grant
Avenue

Hailes Av.
Castlelaw Rd.
Carnethy Av.

Laverockdale Cr.

40

Water of Leith

Road

Woodhall
Road

Campbell
Pk. Dr.
Campbell
Park Cr.

Woodfield

Woodhall
Gro.
Woodhall
Bank

Woodhall

Fernielaw Avenue

Allermuir Rd.
Capelaw Rd.
W. Carnethy Av.

Bonaly
Road

Bonaly Terr.

Bonaly Avenue

Laver.
Loan

Crescent

Laverockdale Pk.

11

Woodhall
Mains

Woodhall

Munro Drive

Bonaly
Steading Drive

Bonaly Gdns.

Bonaly
Bonaly Grove

Bonaly
Wester

Bonaly

Torphin
9 10
10A

627 · Corbie Hill

Bonaly

Bonaly
Brae

Bonaly Rd.

Torphin

Golf Course

Torduff Road

Bonaly
Tower

Road

Bonaly Burn

Torphin Hill

Torphin Hill

Closed to Vehicles

Torduff Hill

Scout Hostel

P

10

Vehicles

Torphin Hill

Torduff
Reservoir

White Hill
1044 ·

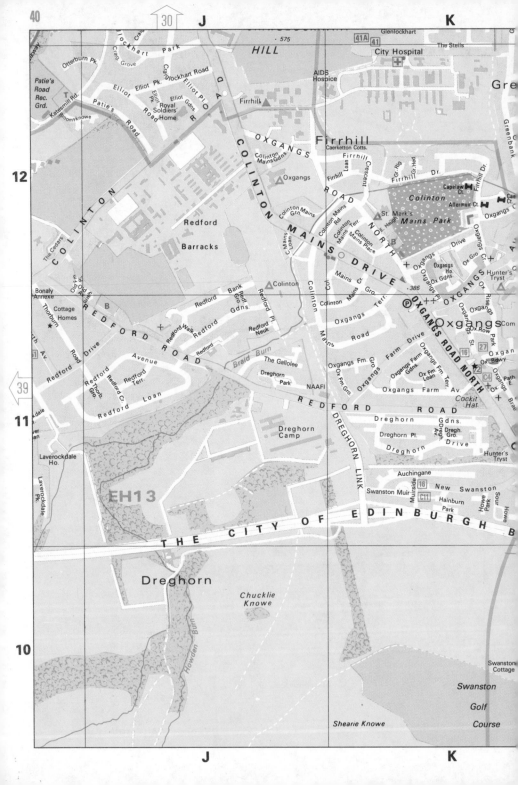

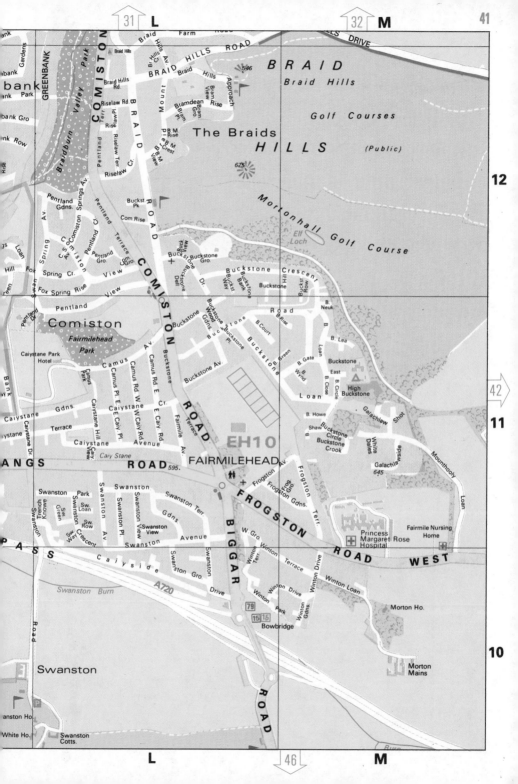

Braid Farm Road
HILLES DRIVE

Braid Hills
Braid Hills Rd.
BRAID HILLS ROAD
Braid
Hills
546

COMISTON Park
GREENBANK
Braidburn Valley Park

bank
Gardens
bank
bank Park
nk Gro
nk Row
Rise
BRAID
Braid Hills

Braid Hills Av.
Riselaw Rd.
Braidmean Gro.
B.M. Rise
B.M. Crest

B R A I D

BRAID
Mount
Bram Rise
Bram View

Braid Hills Approach

Golf Courses

The Braids

HILLS   (Public)

675

BRAID ROAD

Pentland Gdns.
Comiston Springs Av.
Spring
Fox Spring Ct.
Fox Spring Rise
Pentland Ct.
Pentland Terrace
Pentland Gro.
View
View
Comiston Av.
C.S. Av.

Buckst Pk
Com Rise

Buckstone Dr.
Buckstone
Buckstone Gro.
Buckstone Dell

Mortonhall Golf Course
Elf Loch

12

Pentland
Pentland Dr.
Comiston
Fairmilehead Park

Caystane Park Hotel
Caystane Gdns.
Caystane Dr.
stane Dr.

ngs Loan
Hill

Camus Park
Camus Rd. W
Camus Pl. E
Camus Rd.
Caiy Rd.
Caiy Pl.
W.Caiy Rd.
E. Caiy. Rd.

Buckstone
Buckstone Gdns.
Buckstone
Buckstone Av.
Buckstone Pl.
Buckstone

Road
B Rise
B Court
B Green
B Loan
B Neuk
B. Lea
B. Gate
B. Circle
Buckstone East
High Buckstone
B. Close
Buckstone Loan
B. Howe
B Wynd

Galachlaw Shot
White Dales

Galachlawside

42

11

Caystane
Terrace
Caystane Hill
Caystane Hill
Caiy View
Cary Stane

Camus Avenue
Fairmile Terrace

EH10
FAIRMILEHEAD
595.

Frogston Av.
Frogston
Frog Gro.
Frogston Gdns.
Frogston Terr

Shaw
Buckstone Circle
Buckstone Crook
645
Mounthooly Loan

ANGS
PASS

Swanston Park
Sw. Green
Sw. Loan
Trench Knowe
Sw. Row
Sw. Way
Swanston Crescent
Swanston Av.
Swanston Pl.
Swanston View
Swanston Gdns.
Swanston Terr
Swanston View
Swanston
Swanston
Avenue

ROAD
Caiyside
Swanston Burn
A720

BIGGAR ROAD

Swanston Gro.
Swanston Drive

W. Gro.
Winton Terr.
Winton Park
Winton Gdns.
Winton Terrace
Winton Drive
Winton Drive
Winton Loan

FROGSTON ROAD WEST

Princess Margaret Rose Hospital
Fairmile Nursing Home

79
15 15
Bowbridge

Morton Ho.
Morton Mains

10

Swanston

anston Ho.
White Ho.
Swanston Cotts.

Burn

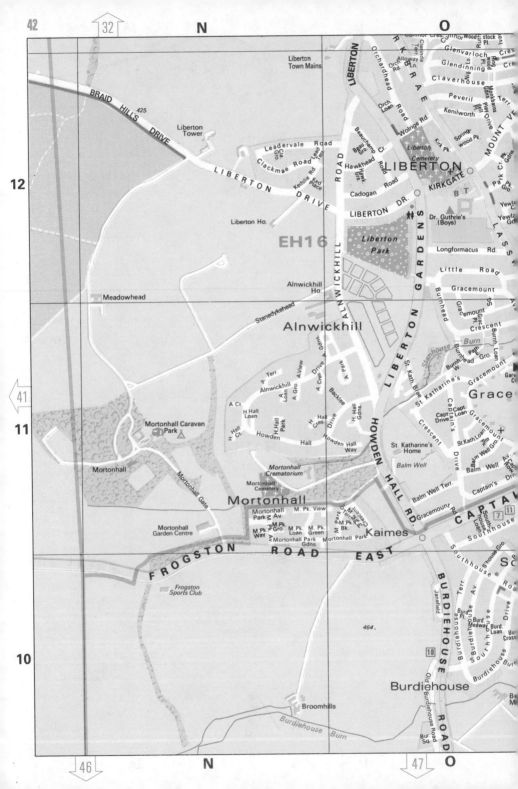

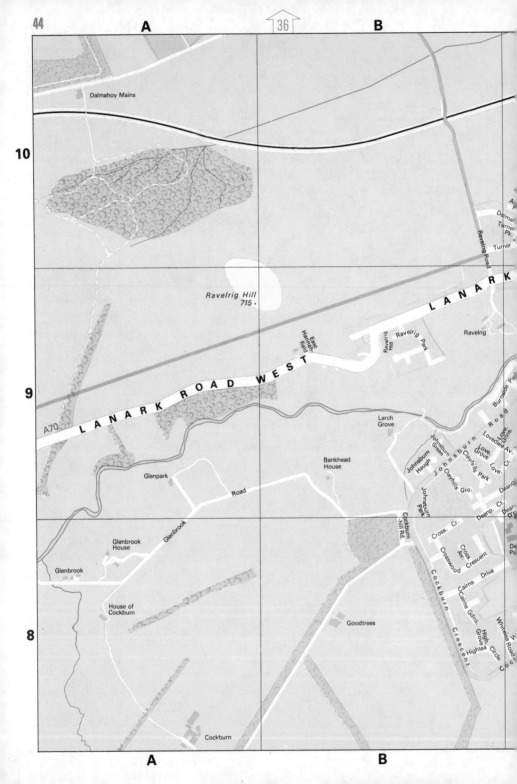

A

B

10

Dalmahoy Mains

Dalmah.
Turner
Pk.

Turner

Ravelrig Road

Turner

Ravelrig Hill
715 ·

L A N A R K

9

East
Hannah-
field

Ravelrig
Hill

Ravelrig
Park

Ravelrig

Ravelrig

Burnside Par

L A N A R K R O A D W E S T

A70

Larch
Grove

R o a d

Love
Gdns.

Lovedale Av.

Love.
Grove

Love.
Ct.

Johnsburn
Green

Johnsburn

ClayHills Park

ClayHills Gro.

Glenpark

Road

Bankhead
House

Johnsburn
Haugh

J o h n s b u r n

Deanp.

Johnsburn
Park

Deanp. Ct.

Dean

De

Glenbrook

Road

Cockburn
hill Rd.

Cross. Cr.

Cross.
Av.

Crosswood

Cross
Crescent

Deanp
Pa

De

Glenbrook
House

Glenbrook

C o c k b u r n

Cairns
Gdns.

Cairns
Drive

Highlea

Whitelea Road

Glenbrook

House of
Cockburn

Goodtrees

C r e s c e n t

High.
Grove

High
Circle

Coc

8

Cockburn

A

B

Currievale

Currie High ★

View

Cr. Pentland

Forth View Rd

View

CU

Newmills Road

Curriehill Castle Drive

Newmills Cr.

Newmills Av. Gr.

Crescent

Cherry Tree Park

Cherry Tree Grove

Cherry Tree Gar.

Currievale Park Grove

Currievale Park

Rowan Tree Av.

Ch.Tr. Av.

Ch.Tr.Loan

Ch.Tr. View Cr.

Rowan Tree Pl.

Ch.Tr.Pl.

Stewart Avenue

Stew. Pl.

Stew. Gr.

Dolphin Gardens West

Dolphin Gardens West

Stew. Cr.

Stew. Gdns.

Dolphin Gdns. E.

Pentland View Ct.

Dolphin

Road

Avenue

Dolphin

Stew. Rd

Waukmill Loan

22

22

B

10

Horsburgh Bk.

Crescent

Horsburgh Gdns.

Old Newmills Road

Newmills Road

Station Loan

LANARK

ROAD

WEST

WEST

ROAD

Water of Leith

Lennox Tower

Lymphoy

Bridge Road

Malleny Park

Balerno High ▲

Bavelaw Road

Dean Park Annexe

P △

Malleny House

Main ★ Lady Ct.

P +

Sawpit Wood

EH 14

9

ALERNO

Dean park Gdns.

Braid

Dean-park Gr.

Mansfield Road

Malleny

D'park Gdns.

Bk.

Harlaw March

Baveław Burn

Harlaw Road

Harlaw

Harlaw Road

Avenue

March. Grove

Threip. Pl.

Threipmuir Gdns.

Threip. Gdns.

Harmeny

The Green

The Lade

Harlaw ▲

8

Crescent

Green. Rd

43

44 74

66 68

Resr.

Malleny Millgate

Balleny †

C

D

L

M

41

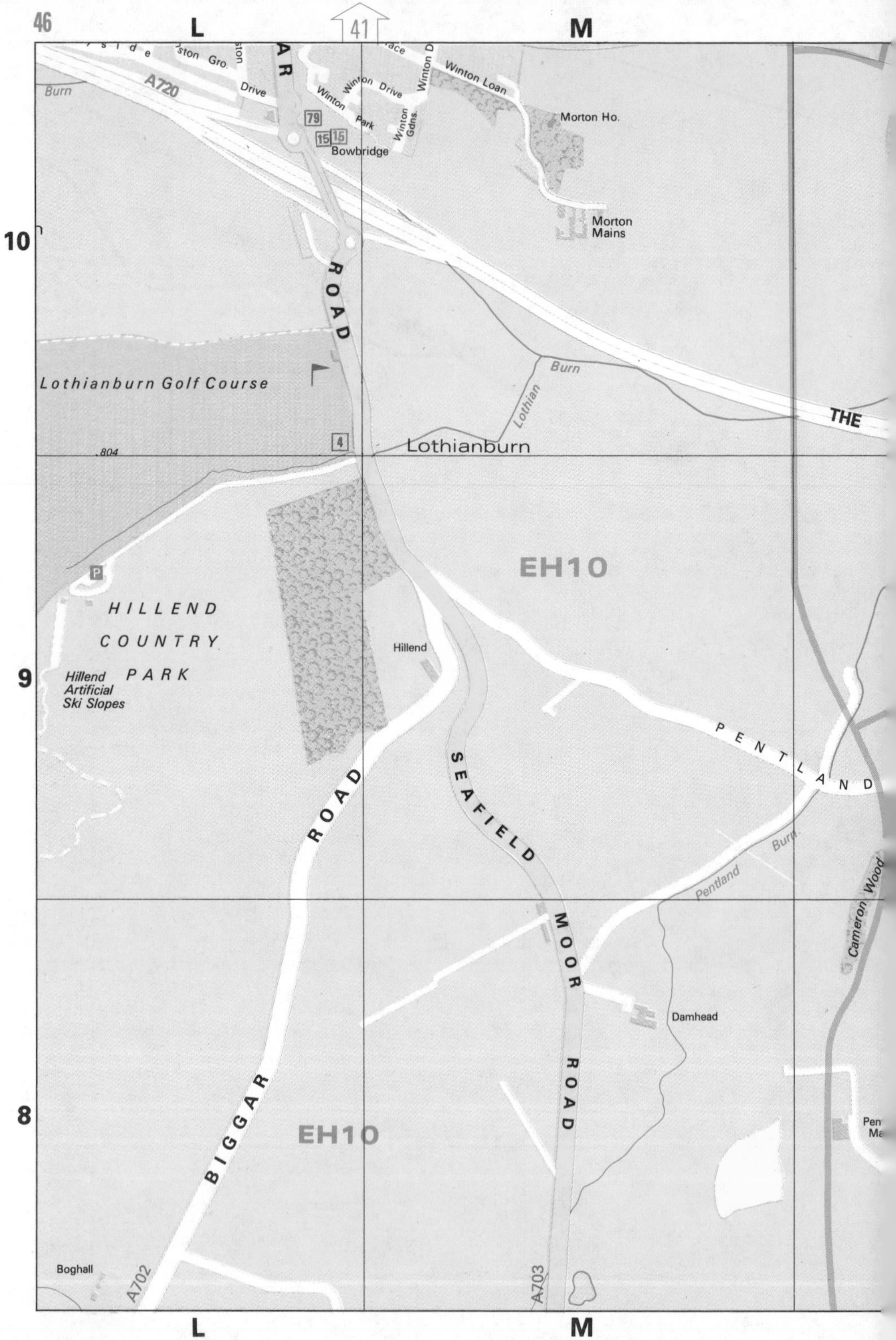

Burn

A720

ston Gro.

Drive

Winton Park

Winton Drive

Winton D

Winton Loan

Winton Gdns.

Terrace

Morton Ho.

79

15 15

Bowbridge

ROAD

10

Morton Mains

Lothianburn Golf Course

Burn

Lothian Burn

THE

.804

4

Lothianburn

EH10

P

HILLEND

COUNTRY

PARK

Hillend

9

Hillend
Artificial
Ski Slopes

SEAFIELD

PENTLAND

ROAD

Pentland Burn

Cameron Wood

MOOR

Damhead

ROAD

8

BIGGAR

EH10

ROAD

Pen
Ma

Boghall

A702

A703

L

M

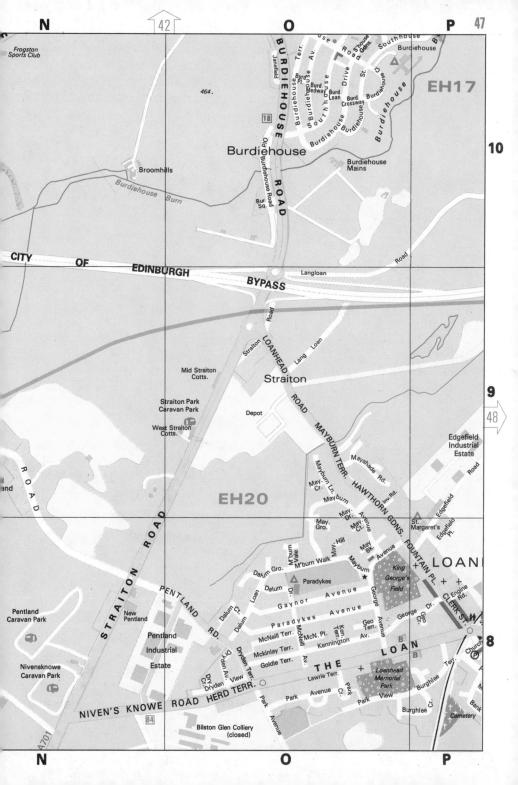

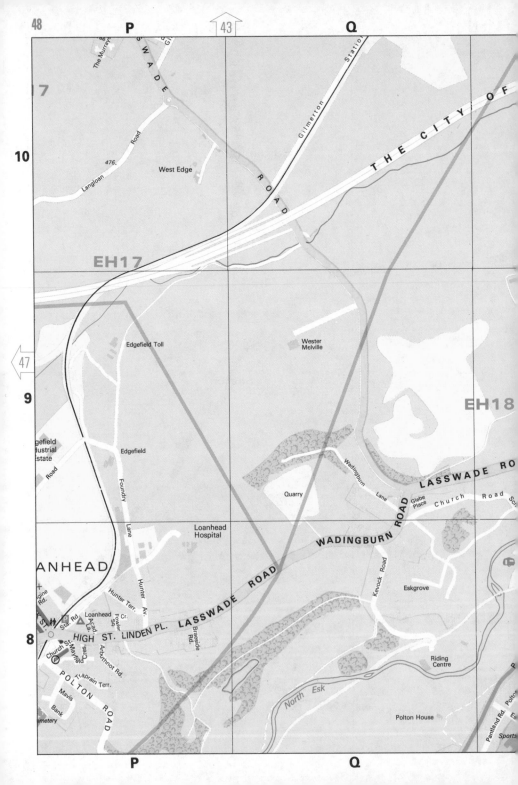

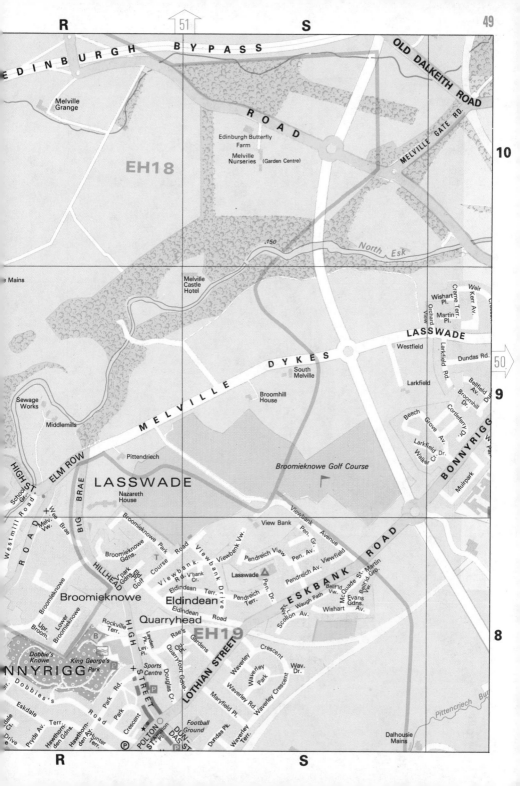

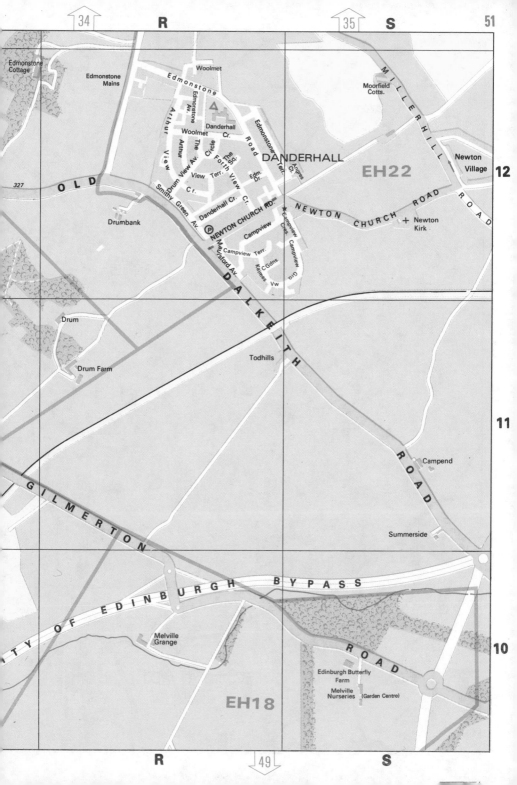

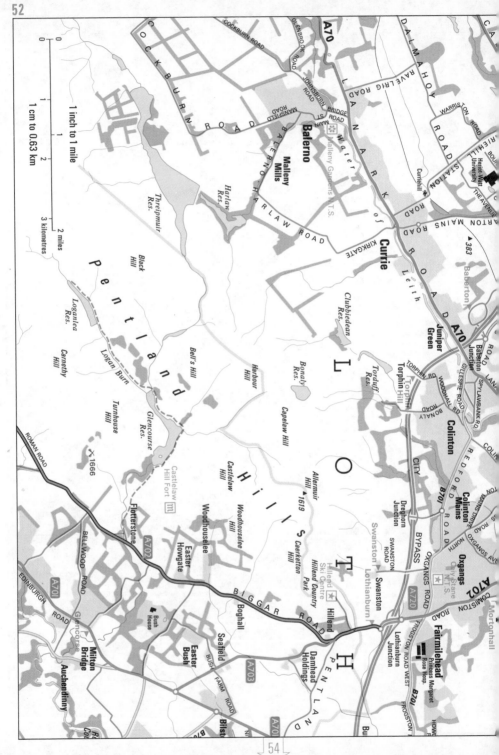

1 inch to 1 mile

0

1

2

3 kilometres

0

1

2 miles

1 cm to 0.63 km

COCKBURN ROAD

GLENBROOK ROAD

COCKBURN ROAD

A70

D A L M A H O Y

RAVELRIG ROAD

WARRISTON ROAD

RIEHMS

HERIOT WATT University

THE AVENUE

RIGHANSTATION

CURRIEHILL

MARTON MAINS ROAD

JOHNSBURN ROAD

BRIDGE ROAD

MANSFIELD ROAD

MAIN ST ROAD

BALERNO

Malleny Mills

Malleny Gardens N.T.S.

Water

BALERNO-HARLAW ROAD

Harlaw Res.

Threipmuir Res.

Black Hill

P e n t l a n d

Loganlea Res.

Carnethy Hill

Logan Burn

Bell's Hill

Turnhouse Hill

Glencorse Res.

Castlelaw Hill Fort

1666

ROMAN ROAD

Flotterstone

A702

BELLWOOD ROAD

EDINBURGH ROAD

A701

Glencorse ROAD

Milton Bridge

Auchendinny

Bush House

Easter Howgate

Woodhouselee

Castlelaw Hill

Woodhouselee Hill

Boghall

BIGGAR ROAD

Seafield

Easter Bush

BUSH FARM ROAD

A703

Bilston

A70

Harbour Hill

Bonaly Res.

Capelaw Hill

H i l l s

Allermuir Hill 1619

S Caerketton Hill

Hillend Ski Centre

Hillend Country Park

Hillend

Boghall

Damhead Holdings

PENTLAND ROAD

Clubbiedean Res.

LANARK ROAD

Water of Leith

KIRKGATE

Currie

Juniper Green

A70

Torduff Res.

Torphin Torphin Hill

TORPHIN RD

WOODHALL ROAD

Colinton

BONALY RD

GILLESPIE ROAD

SPYLAWBANK RD.

Baberton Junction

Baberton

383

L

O

T

H

Dreghorn Junction

Swanston ROAD

Swanston

Lothianburn

Lothianburn Junction

SWANSTON ROAD

City Bypass N.T.S.

Oxgangs

OXGANGS ROAD

OXGANGS AVE

Colinton Mains

REDFORD ROAD

B701

CITY BYPASS

A720

A702

COMISTON ROAD

Fairmilehead

Princess Margaret Rose Hosp.

FROGSTON ROAD WEST

FROGSTON ROAD

B701

Mortonhall

Rifle Park

Union Canal

To Forth Road Bridge

A90

B924

River Almond

EASTFIELD RD

GLASGOW ROAD

Edinburgh Airport (Turnhouse)

NORTON

ROAD

RODDINGLAW ROAD

ADDISTON MAINS

LENNY MUIR

Turnhouse

▲253

CAMMO ROAD

Craigiehall

Cramond Bridge

Barnton Roundabout

CAMMO WALK

Waterfall

Cramond House

Cramond

GLEBE RD

CRAMOND ROAD NORTH

CRAMOND ROAD SOUTH

Cramond Island

FIRTH OF FORTH

Gogarburn Hospital

Gogar

GOGAR STATION ROAD

CITY BYPASS

Gogar Roundabout

GLASGOW ROAD

South Gyle

Maybury Roundabout

North Gyle

MAYBURY ROAD

MAYBURY DRIVE

TURNHOUSE ROAD

QUEENSFERRY ROAD

A902

WHITEHOUSE ROAD

GAMEKEEPER'S ROAD

Royal Burgess

Barnton

Bruntsfield

Moray House College of Education

MARINE DRIVE

Birnie Rocks

Calder Junction

Long

CITY ROAD

HERMISTON ROAD

BANK HEAD DRIVE

Stevenson College of Further Education

South Gyle

S. GYLE RD

CULTINS ROAD

SOUTH GYLE BDWY.

BROOMHOUSE ROAD

B701

Corstorphine

DRUM BRAE SOUTH

DRUM BRAE DRIVE

Queen Margaret Coll. of Education

Clermiston

DRUM BRAE NORTH

B701

SAUGHTON ROAD NORTH

HIGH ST.

ST. JOHN'S ROAD

Corstorphine Hospital

Zoological Park

Corstorphine Castle

CLERMISTON ROAD

CRAIGCROOK ROAD

HILLHOUSE RD

FERRY ROAD

Silverknowes

SILVERKNOWES RD

Muirhouse

MUIRHOUSE PARKWAY

PENNYWELL GARDENS

WEST SHORE ROAD

Sighthill

A71

CALDER ROAD

Napier Polytechnic

SAUGHTON ROAD

Stenhouse

STENHOUSE DRIVE

BROOMHOUSE DRIVE

CITY OF EDINBURGH DISTRICT

Carrick Knowe

Craigcrook

Ravelston

Blackhall

Davidson's Mains

RAVELSTON DYKES ROAD

QUEENSFERRY ROAD

A902

TELFORD ROAD

DRYLAW

Drylaw

GROATHILL ROAD

CREWE ROAD NORTH

MAIN ST.

FERRY RD. NORTH

West Pilton

GRANTON ROAD

PENNYWELL ROAD

Kingsknowe

Longstone

CHESSER AVE

ROYAL

SLATEFORD ROAD

GORGIE ROAD

Murrayfield

Murrayfield Rugby Stadium

Ice Rink

RAVELSTON ROAD

RAVELSTON DYKES

Water of Leith

Gallery of Modern Art

A90

Craigleith

Western General Hospital

CREWE ROAD SOUTH

EAST FETTES AVENUE

B9085

Pilton

Telford Coll. of Further Education

Northern General Hospital

Granton

BOSWALL PARKWAY

GRANTON ROAD

W. HARBOUR ROAD

SEALCARR ST.

W. PIER

ROSEBANK

GRANTON ST.

Granton Harbour

Craiglockhart

Merchants of Edinburgh

Napier Polytechnic

HospItal

GORGIE ROAD

ASHLEY TERR.

POLWORTH TERR.

Hearts F.C.

ROSEBURN

Dalry

WEST

DALRY ROAD

A8

Haymarket

Slateford

GLENLOCKHART ROAD

Hospital

MORNINGSIDE DRIVE

Morningside

COLINTON ROAD

Merchiston

Napier Polytechnic

Royal Edinburgh Hospital

GILMOUR RD.

DUNDEE ST.

FOUNTAINBRIDGE

BREAD ST.

Georgian House N.T.S.

Cath. (Episcopal)

Usher Hall

B900

The Meadows

Comely Bank

INVERLEITH ROW

Royal Botanic Gardens

INVERLEITH PLACE

Inverleith

A902

A903

Powderhall Stadium

Trinity

LOWER GRANTON RD.

E. TRINITY

A901

Newhaven

Leith Docks

MAYFIELD

Blackford

Craigmillar Hill

Royal Observatory

MORNINGSIDE RD.

CLUNY GDNS.

STRATHEARN ROAD

Astley Ainslie Hosp

Bruntsfield Links

MELVILLE DR.

Royal Infirmary

LAURISTON PLACE

Royal Hosp. for Sick Children

GEORGE SQ.

PRINCES STREET

GEORGE STREET

New Town

DUNDAS ST.

Mus. & Art Galleries

Art Gallery

Scott Mon.

Univ. Edin.

Old Town

HOLYROOD

CANONGATE

REGENT ROAD

Calton Hill

G.P.O.

▲328

LONDON RD.

Warriston

BELLEVUE

BROUGHTON RD.

EAST CLAREMONT STREET

LEITH WALK

North Leith

Leith

NEWHAVEN RD.

BONNINGTON RD.

LINDSAY ROAD

NORTH JUNCTION ST.

COMMERCIAL ST.

CRAIGMILLAR

Craigmillar Park ▲539

WEST MAINS RD.

WEST SAVILLE TERR.

GRANGE LOAN

BEAUFORT ROAD

GRANGE ROAD

CLERK ST.

ST. LEONARD'S

PLEASANCE

CAUSEWAYSIDE

QUEEN'S DR.

Newington

BRAIDS

Roslin Glen Country Park
Bilston
B7006
A701
LEADBURN RD
STRATON RD
Burdiehouse
FROGSTON ROAD EAST
HOWDENHALL ROAD
Kaimes
LIBERTON GDNS.
Liberton
LIBERTON DRIVE
A768
NIVEN'S KNOWE RD.
BURDIEHOUSE RD
A701
Gracemount
B701
CAPTAIN'S ROAD
LIBERTON ROAD
ALNWICKHILL

Roslin Chapel
Roslin
THE LOAN
Straiton
B702
HIGH ST.
Straiton Junction
Liberton Hosp.
NEWTOFT ST.
FERNIEHILL DRUM ST.
DYKES STREET
GILMERTON

B1003
Wallace's Cave
POLTON ROAD
EDGEFIELD ROAD
Lasswade Junction
GILMERTON STATION RD.
FERNIEHILL RD.
B701
DRIVE

A6094
Rosewell
POLTON BANK
Loanhead Hosp.
Loanhead
AVENUE RD.
POLTON RD.
LASSWADE ROAD
A720
A7
GILMERTON
Gilmerton
Polton
HIGH ST.
Lasswade
Gilmerton Junction
NEWTON CHURCH RD
A68

St. Joseph's Hospital
POLTON RD.
HIGH ST.
BIG BRAE
MELVILLE DYKES
Broomieknowe
▲336
Sheriffhall Roundabout
A68
MILLERHILL ROAD
Millerhill
OLD DALKEITH RD

MIDLOTHIAN DISTRICT
Dalhousie Burn
COCKPEN ROAD
Bonnyrigg
BONNYRIGG ROAD
A6094
LASSWADE ROAD
A768
River North Esk
A7

B704
Scottish Mining Mus. –Lady Victoria
Eskbank
Terminal College
ESKBANK ROAD
NEW
BATTLE
ABBEY ROAD
Dalkeith Park

A7
Lothianbridge
MURDERDEAN RD.
MAIN STREET
BRYANS ROAD
THE BECHES
ROAD
Newbattle
Newbattle
Easthouses
River South Esk
INVERESK
Dalkeith House
NEWMILLS RD.
ST. ANDREW'S STREET
MUSSELBURGH
Dalkeith

Arniston
ENGINE ROAD
HUNTERFIELD ROAD
STOBHILL ROAD
Newtongrange
BUTTISLEA ROAD
EASTHOUSES ROAD
LAUDER ROAD
A6094
SALTER'S ROAD

B704
STATION ROAD
LADY BRAE
BATTLEKNOWE ROAD
VOGRIE ROAD
Hunterfield
▲790
B6482
ESKVIEW ROAD
BOGWOOD ROAD
WESTHOUSES ROAD

B6372
Newlandrig
Mayfield
Dewartown
Cranstoun Riddel
Whitehill
A68
A612

Country Park
Vogrie House
Edgehead
Cousland
Crossgatehall
1567

EDINBURGH

Holyrood Park
Arthur's Seat ▲823
▲229

QUEEN'S DRIVE

Abbey and Palace of Holyroodhouse

Newington
Mayfield
Craigmillar
Dalkeith Road
Prestonfield
Duddingston
Duddingston Loch
Bingham
Niddrie
Craigmillar
Niddrie Mains Road
Prestonfield

Calton Hill
South Leith
Leith Links
Restalrig
Craigentinny
Seafield Road
Portobello
Joppa
Abercorn Terrace

University
West Mains Road
Cameron Toll Shopping Centre
Inch
Shawfair
Cauldcoats Rd
Whitehill Street
Newcraighall
Newhailes
Musselburgh
Fisherrow
Musselburgh
Monktonhall
Inveresk
Whitecraig
Old Craighall Roundabout
Services

A1
A7
A68
A199
A6095
A6106
A6124
A6094
A1140
A1

FIRTH OF FORTH

Middle Craigs
Eastern Craigs
Black Rocks

Eastern General Hospital
Hibernian F.C.
Meadowbank Sports Centre

Prestonpans
Wallyford
Dolphinstone
Levenhall
Scottish Mining Museum
Royal Musselburgh

East Lothian District
Salters Road
Carberry Road
Edenhall Hospital
Pinkie House

B1348
B6454
B6415
B1361

A199
A900
B900

Abbreviations
Acad.-Academy
Appr.-Approach
Av.-Avenue
Bdgs.-Buildings
Bdwy.-Broadway
Bk.-Bank
Cem.-Cemetery
Cl.-Close
Coll.-College
Cotts.-Cottages
Cr.-Crescent
Crem.-Crematorium
Ct.-Court
Dalk.-Dalkeith inset
Dr.-Drive
E.-East
Er.-Easter
Fm.-Farm
Gall.-Gallery
Gdn.-Garden
Gdns.-Gardens
Gr.-Green
Grd.-Ground
Gro.-Grove
Ho.-House
Hosp.-Hospital
Ind.-Industrial
La.-Lane
Ln.-Loan
Lo.-Lodge
Mem.-Memorial
Muss.-Musselburgh inset
N.-North
Pav.-Pavilion
Pk.-Park
Pl.-Place
Pt.-Port
Qt.-Quadrant
Rd.-Road
S.-South
Sch.-School
Sq.-Square
St.-Saint, Street
Sta.-Station
Terr.-Terrace
Vw.-View
W.-West
Wr.-Wester
Wy.-Way
An asterisk in the index
indicates a street too small to
show on the plan and an
equals sign refers to the
nearest street name.

Consulate Abbreviations

A Austria
Aus Australia
B Belgium
D Germany
DK Denmark
E Spain
F France
GR Greece
I Italy
IS Iceland
N Norway
NL Netherlands
P Portugal
PL Poland
S Sweden
SF Finland
TR Turkey
USA United States of America
VN Vietnam
WAN Nigeria

21 Abbey La. **O17**
50 Abbey Rd., *Dalk.* **T9**
21 Abbey St. **O17**
7 Abbey Strand **N16**
7 Abbeyhill **N16**
7 Abbeyhill Cr. **N17**
21 Abbeyhill Sch. **O17**
7 Abbeymount **N17**

31 Abbotsford Ct. **L14**
31 Abbotsford Cr. **L14**
31 Abbotsford Pk. **L14**
21 Abercorn Av. **P16**
Abercorn Cotts.*=The
Causeway
21 Abercorn Ct. **P16**
21 Abercorn Cr. **P16**
21 Abercorn Dr. **P16**
22 Abercorn Gdns. **P17**
21 Abercorn Gro. **P16**
23 Abercorn Park **S16**
21 Abercorn Rd. **P16**
23 Abercorn Terr. **R16**
6 Abercromby Pl. **M17**
18 Abinger Gdns. **J16**
48 Academy La. **P8**
12 Academy St. **O18**
7 Adam Ho. **M16**
22 Adelphi Gro. **R16**
22 Adelphi Pl. **R16**
45 Addiston Cr. **C10**
44 Addiston Gr. **C10**
36 Addiston Mains **B12**
44 Addiston Pk. **C10**
31 Admiral Terr. **L22**
12 Admiralty St. **N19**
Advocates Cl.*=High St.
Affleck Ct.*=Craigievar
Wynd **N16**
11 Afton Pl. **L19**
11 Afton Terr. **L19**
Agnew Terr.*=Connaught
Pl.
40 AIDS Hospice **J12**
10 Ainslie Park Recreation
Centre **K19**
6 Ainslie Park Sch. **J19**
6 Ainslie Pl. **L17**
7 Air Terminal **M16**
19 Airlie Pl. **M17**
Aitchison's Pl.*=Figgate
St.
30 Aitkenhill **H14**
16 Alan Breck Gdns. **F17**
7 Albany La. **M17**
7 Albany St. **M17**
7 Albany St. La. **M17**
20 Albert Pl. **N17**
13 Albert Rd. **O19**
12 Albert St. **N18**
31 Albert Terr. **L14**
25 Albert Terr., *Muss.* **W15**
21 Albion Pl. **O17**
21 Albion Rd. **O17**
21 Albion Terr. **O17**
6 Albyn Pl. **L17**
30 Alderbank Gdns. **K14**
30 Alderbank Pl. **K14**
30 Alderbank Terr. **K14**
30 Alexander Dr. **J15**
32 Alfred Pl. **N14**
30 Allan Park Cr. **J14**
30 Allan Park Dr. **J13**
30 Allan Park Gdns. **J13**
30 Allan Park Ln. **J13**
30 Allan Park Rd. **J13**
19 Allan St. **L17**
Allandale*=Spylaw St.
H12
20 Allanfield **N17**
50 Allan Terr., *Dalk.* **U10**
40 Allermuir Cr. **K12**
39 Allermuir Rd. **H11**
42 Alloway Ln. **O12**
14 Almond Av. **A16**
Almond Bank
Cotts.*=Whitehouse Rd.
8 Almond Ct. **E18**
16 Almond Gr. **E16**
14 Almond Rd. **A16**
16 Almond Sq. **E16**
30 Almondbank Terr. **K14**
42 Alnwickhill Cr. **N11**
42 Alnwickhill Ct. **N11**
42 Alnwickhill Dr. **N11**
42 Alnwickhill Gdns. **O11**
42 Alnwickhill Gro. **N11**

42 Alnwickhill Ln. **N11**
42 Alnwickhill Pk. **O11**
42 Alnwickhill Rd. **O12**
42 Alnwickhill Terr. **N11**
42 Alnwickhill Vw. **N11**
21 Alva Pl. **O17**
6 Alva St. **L16**
Alvanley
Terr.*=Whitehouse
Loan
19 American Sch., The **L16**
Anchorfield*=Lindsay Rd.
50 Ancrum Bk., *Dalk.* **T9**
50 Ancrum Rd., *Dalk.* **T9**
12 Anderson Pl. **N19**
11 Andrew Wood Ct. **M19**
19 Angle Park Terr. **K15**
51 Angres Ct. **S12**
6 Ann St. **L17**
20 Annandale St. **M18**
20 Annandale St. La. **N17**
12 Annfield **M19**
12 Annfield St. **M19**
7 Antigua St. **N17**
Anworth
Villas*=Saughton Rd. N.
30 Appin Terr. **J14**
7 Appleton Tower **M15**
19 Arboretum Av. **L17**
11 Arboretum Pl. **L18**
11 Arboretum Rd. **L18**
48 Arbuthnot Rd. **P8**
7 Archer's Hall **N15**
6 Archibald Pl. **M16**
32 Arden St. **M15**
31 Ardmillan Pl. **K15**
31 Ardmillan Terr. **K15**
Ardmillan Terr.
La.*=Ardmillan Terr.
16 Ardshiel Av. **F17**
23 Argyle Cr. **R16**
6 Argyle Ho. **M16**
20 Argyle Park Terr. **M15**
20 Argyle Pl. **M15**
12 Argyle St. **N19**
19 Argyll Terr. **L16**
49 Arniston Pl. **R8**
29 Arnott Gdns. **H13**
Arran Pl.*=James St.
23 Arran Pl. **S16**
Arthur Pl.*=Arthur St.
12 Arthur St. **N18**
51 Arthur View Cr. **R12**
51 Arthur View Terr. **R12**
21 Arthur's Seat **O15**
23 Asda Shopping Centre
S15
25 Ashgrove, *Muss.* **W15**
25 Ashgrove Pl., *Muss.* **W15**
25 Ashgrove Vw., *Muss.*
W15
30 Ashley Dr. **K14**
30 Ashley Gdns. **K14**
30 Ashley Gro. **K14**
12 Ashley Pl. **N18**
30 Ashley Terr. **K14**
33 Ashton Gro. **O13**
Ashton Villas*=Brunstane
Rd.
13 Ashville Terr. **O18**
6 Assembly Hall **M16**
6 Assembly Rooms **M16**
12 Assembly St. **O19**
31 Astley Ainslie Hosp. **M14**
6 Atholl Cr. **L16**
6 Atholl Cr. La. **L16**
6 Atholl Pl. **L16**
19 Atholl Terr. **L16**
40 Auchingane **K11**
11 Auchinleck Ct. **M19**
Auchinleck's Brae*=Main
St.
50 Avenue Rd. **T9**
37 Avenue, The **D12**
Avenue Villas*=Crewe Rd.
37 Avenue W. **D11**
17 Aviation Ho. **G15**
8 Avon Gr. **E18**

8 Avon Pl. **E18**
8 Avon Rd. **E18**
19 Avondale Pl. **L17**

38 Baberton Av. **F11**
39 Baberton Cr. **F11**
38 Baberton Golf Course **E11**
38 Baberton Ln. **F11**
38 Baberton Mains **F12**
38 Baberton Mains Av. **F12**
38 Baberton Mains Bk. **F12**
38 Baberton Mains Brae **F12**
38 Baberton Mains Ct. **G12**
38 Baberton Mains Cr. **F12**
38 Baberton Mains Dell **F12**
38 Baberton Mains Dr. **F12**
38 Baberton Mains Gdns.
F12
38 Baberton Mains Gr. **F12**
38 Baberton Mains Gro. **F12**
38 Baberton Mains Hill **F12**
38 Baberton Mains Lea **F12**
39 Baberton Mains Ln. **G12**
38 Baberton Mains Pk. **F12**
38 Baberton Mains Pl. **F12**
38 Baberton Mains Rise **F12**
38 Baberton Mains Row **F12**
38 Baberton Mains Terr. **F12**
39 Baberton Mains Vw. **G12**
38 Baberton Mains Way **F12**
38 Baberton Mains Wood **F12**
38 Baberton Mains Wynd **F12**
38 Baberton Pk. **F11**
38 Baberton Rd. **E12**
38 Baberton Sq. **F11**
19 Back Dean **K17**
42 Backlee **O11**
30 Back Row **J13**
Back Station Rd.*=Peffer
St.
22 Baileyfield Cr. **R16**
22 Baileyfield Rd. **R16**
23 Bailie Gro. **R15**
22 Bailie Path **R15**
23 Bailie Pl. **R15**
22 Bailie Terr. **R15**
18 Baird Av. **J15**
18 Baird Dr. **J15**
18 Baird Gdns. **J15**
18 Baird Gro. **J15**
18 Baird Terr. **J15**
Baker's Pl.*=Kerr St.
18 Balbirnie Pl. **K16**
31 Balcarres Ct. **L13**
25 Balcarres Pl., *Muss.* **V16**
25 Balcarres Rd., *Muss.* **V16**
31 Balcarres St. **K13**
33 Balderston Gdns **O13**
45 Balerno High Sch. **C9**
12 Balfour Pl. **N18**
12 Balfour St. **N18**
16 Balfron Ln. **F17**
17 Balgreen Av. **H15**
17 Balgreen Gdns. **H15**
17 Balgreen Pk. **H15**
17 Balgreen Rd. **J15**
30 Balgreen Sch. **J15**
Ballantyne
La.*=Ballantyne Rd.
12 Ballantyne Rd. **N19**
12 Ballantyne La. **N19**
42 Balm Well Av. **O11**
42 Balm Well Gro. **O11**
42 Balm Well Pk. **O11**
42 Balm Well Terr. **O11**
7 Balmoral Hotel **M16**
19 Balmoral Pl. **L17**
12 Baltic St. **O19**
11 Bangholm Av. **L19**
11 Bangholm Bower Av. **L19**
11 Bangholm Gro. **M19**
11 Bangholm Ln. **M19**
11 Bangholm Pk. **L19**
11 Bangholm Pl. **L30**
11 Bangholm Rd. **L19**
11 Bangholm Terr. **L18**
11 Bangholm Vw. **M19**

Bangholm Villas*=Ferry Rd.
12 Bangor Rd. **N19**
7 Bank of Scotland **M16**
7 Bank St. **M16**
28 Bankhead Av. **F14**
28 Bankhead Bdwy. **E14**
28 Bankhead Crossway N. **E14**
28 Bankhead Crossway S. **E13**
28 Bankhead Dr. **E14, F14**
44 Bankhead Ho. **B9**
28 Bankhead Ln. **F13**
28 Bankhead Medway **F14**
28 Bankhead Pl. **F14**
28 Bankhead St. **F13**
28 Bankhead Terr. **E13**
28 Bankhead Way **E13**
Barclay Pl.*=Bruntsfield Pl.
31 Barclay Terr. **L15**
Barnballoch Ct.*=Craigievar Wynd
39 Barnshot Rd. **H11**
8 Barnton Av. **F18**
8 Barnton Av. W. **E18**
8 Barnton Brae **E18**
16 Barnton Ct. **E18**
9 Barnton Gdns. **G18**
16 Barnton Gro. **E18**
9 Barnton Ln. **G18**
9 Barnton Pk. **G18**
16 Barnton Park Av. **F18**
16 Barnton Park Cr. **F18**
16 Barnton Park Dell **F18**
16 Barnton Park Dr. **F18**
16 Barnton Park Gdns. **F18**
8 Barnton Park Gro. **F18**
16 Barnton Park Pl. **F18**
16 Barnton Park Vw. **F18**
16 Barnton Park Wood **E17**
16 Barnton Thistle Hotel **E18**
16 Barntongate Av. **E17**
16 Barntongate Dr. **E17**
16 Barntongate Terr. **E17**
21 Baronscourt Rd. **P17**
21 Baronscourt Terr. **P17**
7 Barony Pl. **M17**
7 Barony St. **M17**
7 Barony Terr. **F16**
23 Bath Pl. **R17**
13 Bath Rd. **O19**
22 Bath St. **R16**
Bath St. La.*=Bath St.
12 Bathfield **N19**
Baxter's Bdgs.*=Holyrood Rd.
Baxter's Pl.*=Leith Walk
Bavelaw Gdns.*=Bavelaw Rd.
45 Bavelaw Rd. **C9**
22 Beach Lane **R17**
24 Beach La., *Muss.* **U16**
42 Beauchamp Gro. **O12**
42 Beauchamp Rd. **O12**
32 Beaufort Rd. **M14**
11 Beaverbank Pl. **M18**
12 Beaverhall Rd. **M18**
19 Bedford Ct. **L17**
19 Bedford Ct. **L17**
19 Bedford St. **L17**
23 Bedford Terr. **S16**
49 Beech Grove Av. **S9**
17 Beechmount Pk. **H16**
17 Beechwood Mains **H16**
13 Beechwood Terr. **O18**
24 Belfield Av., *Muss.* **U15**
24 Belfield Ct., *Muss.* **U15**
50 Belfield Av. **T9**
19 Belford Av. **K17**
Belford Bridge*=Belford Rd.
19 Belford Gdns. **K17**
19 Belford Mews **K16**
19 Belford Pk. **K16**
19 Belford Pl. **K16**
19 Belford Rd. **K16**

Belford Terr.*=Belford Rd.
19 Belgrave Cr. **K17**
19 Belgrave Cr. La. **K17**
17 Belgrave Gdns. **G16**
19 Belgrave Mews **K17**
17 Belgrave Pl. **K17**
17 Belgrave Rd. **G16**
Belgrave Terr.*=Clermiston Rd.
31 Belhaven Pl. **L13**
31 Belhaven Terr. **L13**
19 Bell Pl. **L17**
33 Bellenden Gdns. **P13**
20 Bellevue **M17**
20 Bellevue Cr. **M17**
20 Bellevue Gdns. **M18**
20 Bellevue Gro. **M17**
20 Bellevue La. **M17**
20 Bellevue Pl. **M17**
20 Bellevue Rd. **M17**
20 Bellevue St. **M17**
20 Bellevue Terr. **M17**
50 Bellfield Av. **T9**
24 Bellfield Av., *Muss.* **U15**
23 Bellfield La. **R16**
23 Bellfield St. **R16**
23 Bellfield Terr. **R16**
49 Bellfield Vw. **S8**
19 Bells Brae **L16**
Bell's Mills*=Belford Rd.
Bell's Wynd*=High St.
17 Belmont Av. **H16**
17 Belmont Cr. **H16**
17 Belmont Gdns. **H16**
17 Belmont Pk. **H16**
38 Belmont Rd. **F11**
17 Belmont Terr. **H16**
18 Belmont Vw. **H16**
11 Belvedere Pk. **M19**
11 Beresford Av. **M19**
11 Beresford Gdns. **M19**
11 Beresford Pl. **L19**
11 Beresford Terr. **M19**
12 Bernard St. **O19**
20 Bernard Terr. **N15**
Berry Sq.*=Figgate St.
25 Beulah, *Muss.* **W15**
50 Bevan Lee Ct., *Dalk.* **U10**
49 Big Brae **R8**
46 Biggar Rd. **L8**
47 Bilston Glen Colliery **O8**
22 Bingham Av. **Q15**
34 Bingham Bdwy. **Q15**
34 Bingham Cr. **R15**
34 Bingham Crossway **Q15**
34 Bingham Dr. **Q15**
34 Bingham Medway **Q15**
22 Bingham Pk. **Q15**
34 Bingham Pl. **Q15**
34 Bingham St. **Q15**
34 Bingham Way **Q15**
16 Birch Ct. **E17**
9 Birnies Ct. **H19**
32 Blacket Av. **N15**
32 Blacket Pl. **N15**
33 Blackbarony Rd. **O13**
35 Blackchapel Rd. **R14**
32 Blackford Av. **M14**
32 Blackford Bk. **M14**
32 Blackford Glen Rd. **N13**
32 Blackford Hill **M13**
32 Blackford Hill Gro. **M13**
32 Blackford Hill Rise **M13**
32 Blackford Hill Vw. **M13**
32 Blackford Rd. **M14**
7 Blackfriars St. **N16**
13 Blackhall Sch. **H17**
16 Blackthorn Ct. **E17**
32 Blackwood Cr. **N15**
16 Blaeberry Gdns. **E17**
20 Blair St. **M16**
31 Blantyre Terr. **L14**
12 Bleachfield **M19**
7 Blenheim Pl. **N17**
18 Blinkbonny Av. **J17**
18 Blinkbonny Cr. **J17**

18 Blinkbonny Gdns. **J17**
18 Blinkbonny Gro. **J17**
18 Blinkbonny Gro. W. **J17**
18 Blinkbonny Rd. **J17**
38 Blinkbonny Rd., *Currie* **E10**
18 Blinkbonny Terr. **J17**
38 Bloomiehall Pk. **F11**
11 Boat Gr. **M18**
46 Boghall **L8**
24 Bog Park Rd., *Muss.* **U15**
29 Bogsmill Rd. **H13**
39 Bonaly Annexe **H12**
39 Bonaly Av. **H11**
39 Bonaly Brae **H11**
39 Bonaly Cr. **H11**
39 Bonaly Dr. **H11**
39 Bonaly Gdns. **H11**
39 Bonaly Gro. **H11**
39 Bonaly Rise **H11**
39 Bonaly Rd. **H11**
39 Bonaly Sch. **H10**
39 Bonaly Sch. Annexe **H12**
39 Bonaly Steading **H11**
39 Bonaly Terr. **H11**
39 Bonaly Tower **H10**
39 Bonaly Wester **H11**
12 Bonar Pl. **M19**
12 Bonnington Av. **M19**
12 Bonnington Gro. **M19**
12 Bonnington Rd. **N18**
12 Bonnington Rd. La. **N18**
12 Bonnington Sch. **N18**
12 Bonnington Sch. Annexe **N19**
12 Bonnington Terr. **M19**
12 Bonnyhaugh **M18**
12 Bonnyhaugh La. **M18**
50 Bonnyrigg Rd. **T9**
Boothacre Cotts.*=Seafield Pl.
13 Boothacre La. **P18**
Boroughloch Bdgs.*=Boroughloch Sq.
7 Boroughloch La. **N15**
Boroughloch Sq.*=Boroughloch La.
19 Borthwick Pl. **K16**
Borthwick's Cl.*=High St.
11 Boswall Av. **K19**
11 Boswall Cr. **K19**
10 Boswall Dr. **K19**
11 Boswall Gdns. **K19**
11 Boswall Gr. **L19**
11 Boswall Gro. **K19**
11 Boswall Ln. **K19**
10 Boswall Parkway **K19**
11 Boswall Pl. **K19**
11 Boswall Qt. **K19**
11 Boswall Rd. **L19**
11 Boswall Sq. **K19**
11 Boswall Terr. **K19**
21 Bothwell St. **O17**
37 Boundary Rd. **D12**
41 Bowbridge **L10**
11 Bowhill Terr. **L18**
12 Bowie's Cl. **O19**
12 Bowling Gr., The **N19**
7 Bowmont Pl. **N15**
Boyd's Entry*=St. Mary's St.
8 Brae Pk. **E18**
8 Brae Park Rd. **D18**
33 Braefoot Terr. **O13**
8 Braehead Av. **E18**
8 Braehead Bk. **E18**
8 Braehead Cr. **E18**
8 Braehead Dr. **E18**
8 Braehead Gro. **E18**
8 Braehead Ln. **E18**
8 Braehead Pk. **E18**
8 Braehead Rd. **E18**
Braehead Row*=Braehead Av.
8 Braehead Vw. **E18**

48 Braeside Rd. **P8**
8 Braepark Rd. **E18**
31 Braid Av. **L13**
31 Braid Cr. **L13**
31 Braid Farm Rd. **L13**
42 Braid Hills **M12**
31 Braid Hills Approach **L12**
31 Braid Hills Av. **L13**
31 Braid Hills Cr. **L12**
32 Braid Hills Dr. **M13**
41 Braid Hills Golf Course **M12**
41 Braid Hills Hotel **L12**
41 Braid Hills Rd. **L12**
41 Braid Mount **L12**
41 Braid Mt. Crest **L12**
41 Braid Mt. Rise **L12**
41 Braid Mt. Vw. **L12**
31 Braid Rd. **L12**
31 Braidburn Cr. **L13**
31 Braidburn Terr. **L13**
41 Braidburn Valley Pk. **L12**
16 Bramble Dr. **E17**
41 Bramdean Gro. **L12**
41 Bramdean Pl. **L12**
41 Bramdean Rise **L12**
41 Bramdean Vw. **L12**
26 Brampton Lodge **B13**
23 Brand Dr. **R15**
23 Brand Gdns. **S16**
Brand Pl.*=Abbeyhill
6 Brandfield St. **L15**
20 Brandon St. **M17**
20 Brandon Terr. **M17**
7 Brass Rubbing Centre **N16**
6 Bread St. **L16**
Bread St. La.*=Bread St.
19 Bread Terr. **L16**
12 Breadalbane St. **N19**
19 Breadalbane Terr. **L16**
Brewery La.*=Great Junction St.
30 Briarbank Terr. **K14**
Brickfield*=Pipe St.
Brickwork Cl.*=Giles St.
33 Bridge End **O14**
19 Bridge Pl. **L17**
39 Bridge Rd. **H11**
19 Bridge Rd. **C9**
22 Bridge St. **R17**
22 Bridge St. La. **R17**
25 Bridge St., *Muss.* **V15**
7 Briery Bauks **N15**
19 Bright Terr. **L16**
22 Brighton Pk **R16**
11 Brighton Pl. **R16**
7 Brighton St. **M16**
32 Bright's Cr. **N14**
7 Bristo Pl. **M16**
7 Bristo Port **M16**
7 Bristo Sq. **M16**
32 British Geological Survey **M14, N13**
22 Britwell Cr. **P17**
12 Broad Wynd **O19**
29 Broombank Terr. **F14**
29 Broomburn Gro. **G15**
19 Broomfield Cr. **G14**
29 Broomhall Av. **F14**
28 Broomhall Bk. **F15**
28 Broomhall Dr. **F15**
28 Broomhall Gdns. **F15**
28 Broomhall Ln. **F15**
28 Broomhall Pk. **F15**
28 Broomhall Pl. **F15**
28 Broomhall Rd. **F15**
28 Broomhall Terr. **F15**
49 Broomhill Dr. **T9**
49 Broomhill Ho. **S9**
42 Broomhills **M10**
29 Broomhouse Av. **F14**
29 Broomhouse Bk. **G14**
29 Broomhouse Cotts. E. **G14**
29 Broomhouse Cotts. W. **F14**
29 Broomhouse Ct. **G14**
29 Broomhouse Cr. **G14**
29 Broomhouse Dr. **F14**

29 Broomhouse Gdns. **F14**
29 Broomhouse Gdns. E. **G14**
29 Broomhouse Gdns. W. **F14**
29 Broomhouse Gro. **G14**
29 Broomhouse Ln. **G14**
29 Broomhouse Market **G14**
29 Broomhouse Medway **G14**
29 Broomhouse Pk. **F14**
29 Broomhouse Path **F14**
29 Broomhouse Pl. N. **F14**
29 Broomhouse Pl. S. **G14**
28 Broomhouse Rd. **F14**
29 Broomhouse Row **G14**
29 Broomhouse Sch. **G14**
29 Broomhouse Sq. **G14**
29 Broomhouse St. N. **F14**
29 Broomhouse St. S. **G13**
29 Broomhouse Terr. **G14**
29 Broomhouse Walk **G14**
29 Broomhouse Way **G14**
29 Broomhouse Wynd **G14**
49 Broomieknowe **R8**
49 Broomieknowe Gdns. **R8**
49 Broomieknowe Golf Course **S9**
49 Broomieknowe Pk. **R8**
29 Broomlea Cr. **F15**
29 Broompark Rd. **F15**
29 Broomside Terr. **G15**
29 Broomview Ho. **F13**
40 Broomyknowe **H12**
6 Brougham Pl. **M15**
6 Brougham St. **L15**
7 Broughton Market **M17**
20 Broughton Pl. **M17**
12 Broughton Rd. **M18**
12 Broughton Sch. **M18**
19 Broughton Sch. (Sec.) **K17**
7 Broughton St. **M17**
7 Broughton St. La. **M17**
7 Brown St. **N22**
Brown's Cl.*=Canongate
Brown's Pl.*=Vennel
50 Bruce Gdns., *Dalk.* **U9**
31 Bruce St. **L13**
23 Brunstane Bk. **S15**
23 Brunstane Cr. **S15**
23 Brunstane Dr. **S15**
23 Brunstane Gdns. **S16**
Brunstane Gdns. Mews*=Brunstane Gdns.
23 Brunstane Rd. **S16**
23 Brunstane Rd. N. **S16**
23 Brunstane Rd. S. **S15**
23 Brunstane Sch. **S15**
23 Brunstanegate **S15**
20 Brunswick Pl. **N17**
20 Brunswick Rd. **N17**
20 Brunswick St. **N17**
20 Brunswick St. La. **N17**
Brunton Gdns.*=Montgomery St.
25 Brunton Hall and Theatre, *Muss.* **V15**
20 Brunton Pl. **N17**
20 Brunton Terr. **N17**
Brunton's Cl.*=High St.
31 Bruntsfield Av. **L15**
31 Bruntsfield Cr. **L15**
31 Bruntsfield Gdns. **L15**
8 Bruntsfield Golf Course **F19**
31 Bruntsfield Health Centre **L15**
31 Bruntsfield Hotel **L15**
32 Bruntsfield Links **L15**
31 Bruntsfield Pl. **L15**
31 Bruntsfield Sch. **L15**
31 Bruntsfield Terr. **L15**
22 Bryce Av. **Q17**
38 Bryce Cr. **E11**
Bryce Gdns.*=Bryce Rd.
22 Bryce Gro. **Q17**
38 Bryce Pl. **E11**
38 Bryce Rd. **E11**

31 Bryson Rd. **K15**
7 Buccleuch Pl. **M15**
7 Buccleuch St. **N15**
50 Buccleuch St., *Dalk.* **U10**
20 Buccleuch Terr. **N15**
12 Buchanan St. **N18**
19 Buckingham Terr. **K17**
41 Buckstane Park **L12**
41 Buckstone Av. **L11**
41 Buckstone Bk. **L12**
41 Buckstone Circle **M11**
41 Buckstone Circle S. **M11**
41 Buckstone Cl. **M11**
41 Buckstone Ct. **L11**
41 Buckstone Cr. **L12**
41 Buckstone Crook **M11**
41 Buckstone Dell **L12**
41 Buckstone Dr. **L12**
41 Buckstone Gdns. **L11**
41 Buckstone Gate **M11**
41 Buckstone Gr. **L11**
41 Buckstone Gro. **L12**
41 Buckstonehead **M11**
41 Buckstone Hill **L12**
41 Buckstone Howe **M11**
41 Buckstone Lea **M11**
41 Buckstone Ln. **L15**
41 Buckstone Ln. E. **M11**
41 Buckstone Neuk **M11**
41 Buckstone Pl. **L11**
41 Buckstone Rise **M11**
41 Buckstone Rd. **L11**
41 Buckstone Row **M12**
41 Buckstone Sch. **M11**
41 Buckstone Shaw **M11**
Buckstoneside*= Buckstone Circle
41 Buckstone Terr. **L11**
41 Buckstone Vw. **L12**
41 Buckstone Way **L12**
41 Buckstone Wood **L11**
41 Buckstone Wynd **M11**
16 Bughtlin Dr. **E17**
16 Bughtlin Gdns. **E16**
16 Bughtlin Gr. **E16**
16 Bughtlin Ln. **E16**
16 Bughtlin Market **E16**
16 Bughtlin Pk. **E16**
16 Bughtlin Pl. **E17**
7 Bull's Cl. **N16**
42 Burdiehouse Av. **O10**
43 Burdiehouse Burn Pk. **P10**
43 Burdiehouse Cr. **O10**
42 Burdiehouse Crossway **O10**
42 Burdiehouse Dr. **O10**
42 Burdiehouse Ln. **O10**
42 Burdiehouse Medway **O10**
42 Burdiehouse Pl. **O10**
42 Burdiehouse Rd. **O10**
43 Burdiehouse Sch. **O10**
42 Burdiehouse Sq. **O10**
42 Burdiehouse St. **O10**
42 Burdiehouse Terr. **O10**
12 Burgess St. **O19**
33 Burgess Terr. **O14**
47 Burghlee Cr. **P8**
47 Burghlee Terr. **P8**
43 Burghtoft **Q18**
12 Burlington St. **N19**
16 Burnbrae **E16**
42 Burnhead Cr. **O11**
42 Burnhead Gro. **O11**
42 Burnhead Ln. **O11**
42 Burnhead Path E. **O11**
42 Burnhead Path W. **O11**
12 Burns St. **O18**
16 Burnside **E16**
44 Burnside Pk. **B9**
24 Bush St., *Muss.* **U16**
24 Bush Terr., *Muss.* **U15**
7 Bus Sta. **M17**

12 Cables Wynd **N19**
12 Cables Wynd Ho. **N19**
8 Caddell's Row **E19**
12 Cadiz St. **O19**

42 Cadogan Rd. **O12**
21 Cadzow Pl. **O17**
40 Caerketton Cotts. **K12**
40 Caerketton Ct. **K12**
Caerlaverock Ct.*=Craigievar Wynd
24 Cairds Row, *Muss.* **U16**
7 Cairn Hotel **N17**
44 Cairns Dr. **B8**
44 Cairns Gdns. **B8**
12 Cairngorm Ho. **N19**
17 Cairnmuir Rd. **G16**
30 Cairnpark Sch. **H13**
33 Cairntows Close **P14**
Caithness Pl.*=Clark Rd.
11 Caithness Pl. **L19**
41 Caiy Stane **L11**
41 Cayside **L10**
41 Caiystane Av. **L11**
41 Caiystane Cr. **L11**
41 Caiystane Dr. **K11**
41 Caiystane Gdns. **K11**
41 Caiystane Hill **L11**
41 Caiystane Pk. Hotel **L11**
41 Caiystane Terr. **K11**
41 Caiystane Vw. **L11**
28 Calder Ct. **F13**
28 Calder Cr. **E13**
28 Calder Dr. **F13**
28 Calder Gdns. **E13**
28 Calder Gro. **F13**
28 Calder Pk. **F13**
28 Calder Pl. **F13**
36 Calder Rd. **A12**
29 Calder Rd. Gdns. **H14**
28 Calder Vw. **E13**
19 Caledonian Cr. **K22**
19 Caledonian Hotel **L16**
19 Caledonian Pl. **K15**
19 Caledonian Rd. **L15**
7 Calton Hill **N17**
7 Calton Hill (Street) **N17**
7 Calton New Burial Ground **N17**
7 Calton Rd. **N16**
12 Cambridge Av. **N18**
12 Cambridge Gdns. **N18**
6 Cambridge St. **L16**
6 Cambridge St. La. **L16**
21 Cambusnethan St. **O17**
6 Cameo Cinema **L15**
33 Cameron Cr. **O14**
33 Cameron Ho. Av **O14**
33 Cameron Pk. **O14**
37 Cameron Smail Rd. **D12**
33 Cameron Toll **O14**
33 Cameron Toll Gdns. **O14**
33 Cameron Toll Shopping Centre **O14**
16 Cammo Bk. **E17**
16 Cammo Brae **E17**
16 Cammo Cr. **E17**
16 Cammo Gdns. **E17**
16 Cammo Gro. **D17**
16 Cammo Hill **D17**
16 Cammo Home Farm **D17**
16 Cammo Parkway **E17**
16 Cammo Pl. **E17**
15 Cammo Rd. **C17**
16 Cammo Walk **D17**
18 Campbell Av. **J16**
39 Campbell Pk. **G11**
39 Campbell Park Cr. **G11**
39 Campbell Park Dr. **G11**
18 Campbell Rd. **J16**
Campbell's Cl.*=Calton Rd.
Campie Court*=Campie Gdns.
24 Campie Gdns., *Muss.* **U15**
24 Campie La., *Muss.* **U15**
24 Campie Rd., *Muss.* **U15**
24 Campie Sch., *Muss.* **U15**
51 Campview **R12**
51 Campview Av. **R12**
51 Campview Cr. **R12**

51 Campview Gdns. **R12**
51 Campview Gro. **S12**
49 Campview Rd. **R8**
51 Campview Terr. **R12**
41 Camus Av. **L11**
41 Camus Pk. **L11**
41 Camus Pl. E. **L11**
41 Camus Rd. E. **L11**
41 Camus Rd. W. **L11**
31 Canaan Home **L14**
41 Canaan La. **L14**
31 Canaan Lodge **L14**
7 Candlemaker Row **M16**
43 Candlemaker's Cr. **Q11**
43 Candlemaker's Pk. **Q11**
6 Canning St. **L16**
6 Canning St. La. **L16**
6 Cannon Film Centre **L16**
12 Cannon Wynd **N19**
20 Canon La. **M17**
20 Canon St. **M17**
7 Canongate **N16**
20 Canonmills **M18**
31 Canonmills Sch. **M17**
40 Capelaw Ct. **K12**
39 Capelaw Rd. **H11**
17 Capital Hotel **G17**
42 Captain's Dr. **O11**
42 Captain's Ln. **O11**
42 Captain's Rd. **O11**
42 Captain's Row **O11**
18 Carberry Pl. **K16**
25 Carberry Rd., *Muss.* **V14**
17 Carfrae Gdns. **H17**
17 Carfrae Gro. **H17**
17 Carfrae Pk. **H17**
18 Carfrae Rd. **H17**
11 Cargil Ct. **L19**
11 Cargil Terr. **L19**
8 Cargilfield Sch. **E18**
32 Carlton Cricket Grd. **M14**
7 Carlton Highland Hotel **M16**
6 Carlton St. **L17**
7 Carlton Terr. **N17**
7 Carlton Terr. La. **N17**
7 Carlton Terr. Mews **N17**
21 Carlyle Pl. **O17**
24 Carlyle Pl., *Muss.* **V15**
7 Carnegie Ct. **N16**
39 Carnethy Av. **H11**
17 Caroline Gdns. **G16**
10 Caroline Pk. **J20**
10 Caroline Park Av. **J20**
10 Caroline Park Gro. **J19**
17 Caroline Pl. **G16**
16 Caroline Terr. **F16**
Carpet La.*=Bernard St.
50 Carrick Cr., *Dalk.* **V8**
29 Carrick Knowe Av. **G15**
29 Carrick Knowe Dr. **G15**
29 Carrick Knowe Gdns. **G15**
29 Carrick Knowe Golf Course **H15**
29 Carrick Knowe Gro. **G15**
29 Carrick Knowe Hill **G15**
29 Carrick Knowe Ln. **G15**
29 Carrick Knowe Parkway **G15**
29 Carrick Knowe Pl. **G15**
29 Carrick Knowe Rd. **G14**
29 Carrick Knowe Sch. **G15**
29 Carrick Knowe Terr. **G15**
Carrington Cr.*=Crewe Rd.
19 Carrington Rd. **K17**
13 Carron Pl. **O19**
Carruber's Cl.*=High St.
12 Casselbank St. **N18**
12 Cassel's La. **N18**
6 Castle **M16**
29 Castle Av. **F15**
6 Castle Esplanade **M16**
15 Castle Gogar **C16**
6 Castle St. **L16**
6 Castle Terr. **L16**
20 Castle Wynd N. **M16**
20 Castle Wynd S. **M16**

34 Castlebrae Sch. **Q14**
34 Castlebrae Sch. Annexe **Q14**
6 Castlehill **M16**
39 Castlelaw Rd. **H11**
33 Castleview Ho. **P12**
13 Cat & Dog Home **Q18**
19 Cathcart Pl. **K15**
7 Cathedral La. **M17**
11 Catherine Pl. **M18**
Catherine Pl.*= Canonmills
30 Cattle Rd. **H14**
35 Cauldcoats **R13**
21 Causeway, The **P15**
32 Causewayside **N15**
22 Cavalry Park Dr. **P15**
39 Cedars, The **H12**
7 Central Library **M16**
Chalmers Bdgs.*=Fountainbridge
Chalmers Cl.*=High St.
32 Chalmers Cr. **M15**
6 Chalmers Hosp. **M16**
20 Chalmers St. **M15**
31 Chamberlain Rd. **L14**
7 Chambers St. **M16**
25 Champigny Ct., *Muss.* **W15**
12 Chancelot Cr. **M19**
11 Chancelot Gro. **M19**
12 Chancelot Mills **N20**
12 Chancelot Terr. **M19**
34 Chapel Ct. **Q14**
Chapel La.*=Maritime St.
7 Chapel St. **N15**
Chapel Wynd*=West Port
Charlesfield*=Bristo Sq.
7 Charles St. **M16**
7 Charles St. La. **M23**
6 Charlotte La. **L16**
6 Charlotte Sq. **L16**
32 Charterhall Gro. **M14**
32 Charterhall Rd. **M13**
45 Cherry Tree Av. **C10**
45 Cherry Tree Cr. **D10**
45 Cherry Tree Gdns. **C10**
45 Cherry Tree Gro. **C10**
45 Cherry Tree Ln. **D10**
45 Cherry Tree Pk. **C10**
45 Cherry Tree Vw. **D10**
20 Chessels Ct. **N16**
30 Chesser Av. **H14**
Chesser Cotts.*=Gorgie Rd.
30 Chesser Cr. **J14**
30 Chesser Gdns. **H14**
30 Chesser Gro. **H14**
30 Chesser Ho. **H14**
30 Chesser Ln. **H14**
6 Chester St. **L16**
10 Chestnut St. **K20**
19 Cheyne St. **L17**
23 Christian Cr. **R16**
23 Christian Gro. **R16**
22 Christian Path **R16**
22 Christiemiller Av. **Q17**
22 Christiemiller Gro. **Q17**
22 Christiemiller Pl. **Q17**
31 Church Hill **L14**
31 Church Hill Pl. **L14**
31 Church Hill Theatre **L14**
31 Church Hill Dr. **L14**
24 Church La., *Muss.* **V15**
48 Church Rd. **Q9**
47 Church St. **P8**
25 Church St. **V15**
51 Circle, The **R12**
6 Circus Gdns. **L17**
6 Circus La. **L17**
12 Citadel Ct. **N19**
12 Citadel St. **N19**
Citadel Pl.*=Commercial St.
7 City Art Centre **M16**
7 City Chambers **M16**
30 City Hosp. **K12**
7 City Observatory **N17**

27 City of Edinburgh By Pass **D14**
9 Civil Service Sports Grd. **H19**
42 Clackmae Gro. **N12**
42 Clackmae Rd. **N12**
33 Clapper La. **O13**
Clapperton Pl.*=Lower London Rd.
13 Clarebank Cr. **O18**
12 Claremont Bk. **M17**
12 Claremont Ct. **M18**
12 Claremont Cr. **M29**
13 Claremont Gdns. **O18**
12 Claremont Gro. **M18**
13 Claremont Pk. **O18**
13 Claremont Rd. **O18**
19 Clarence St. **L17**
19 Clarendon Cr. **L17**
19 Clarendon Hotel **L16**
50 Clarinda Gdns., *Dalk.* **V9**
33 Clarinda Terr. **O13**
14 Clark Av. **M19**
11 Clark Pl. **L19**
11 Clark Rd. **L19**
33 Claverhouse Dr. **O12**
44 Clayhills Gro. **B9**
44 Clayhills Pk. **B9**
24 Clayknowes Dr., *Muss.* **T15**
24 Clayknowes Pl., *Muss.* **U15**
24 Clayknowes Rd., *Muss.* **U15**
24 Clayknowes Wy., *Muss.* **U15**
33 Clearburn Cr. **O14**
33 Clearburn Gdns. **O14**
33 Clearburn Rd. **O14**
34 Cleekim Dr. **R14**
34 Cleekim Rd. **R14**
35 Cleikiminfield **R14**
35 Cleikiminrig **R14**
20 Clerk St. **N15**
47 Clerk St. **P8**
16 Clermiston Av. **F17**
16 Clermiston Cr. **F17**
16 Clermiston Dr. **F17**
17 Clermiston Gdns. **F17**
16 Clermiston Gr. **F17**
17 Clermiston Gro. **F17**
17 Clermiston Hill **F17**
16 Clermiston Ln. **F17**
17 Clermiston Medway **F17**
16 Clermiston Pk. (st.) **F17**
17 Clermiston Pl. **F17**
17 Clermiston Rd. **G16**
17 Clermiston Rd. N. **G17**
16 Clermiston Sch. **F17**
16 Clermiston Terr. **G16**
17 Clermiston Vw. **G17**
16 Clerwood Bk. **F16**
16 Clerwood Gdns. **F16**
16 Clerwood Gro. **F16**
16 Clerwood Ln. **F16**
17 Clerwood Pk. **F16**
16 Clerwood Pl. **G16**
16 Clerwood Row **F16**
17 Clerwood Terr. **G16**
17 Clerwood Vw. **G16**
16 Clerwood Way **F16**
Clifton Sq.*=Baileyfield Rd.
19 Clifton Terr. **L16**
31 Clinton Rd. **L14**
21 Clockmill La. **O17**
39 Clovenstone Dr. **G12**
39 Clovenstone Gdns. **G12**
39 Clovenstone Pk. **G12**
39 Clovenstone Rd. **G12**
39 Clovenstone Sch. **G12**
31 Cluny Av. **L13**
31 Cluny Dr. **L13**
31 Cluny Gdns. **L13**
31 Cluny Pl. **M14**
31 Cluny Terr. **L13**
7 Clyde St. **M17**

12 Coalhill **N19**
6 Coates Cr. **L16**
19 Coates Gdns. **K16**
19 Coates Pl. **L16**
12 Coatfield La. **O19**
28 Cobbinshaw Ho. **F13**
32 Cobden Cr. **N14**
32 Cobden Rd. **N14**
19 Cobden Terr. **L16**
12 Coburg St. **N19**
Cochran Pl.*=East London St.
20 Cochran Terr. **M17**
13 Cochrane Pl. **O18**
37 Cockburn **A8**
44 Cockburn Cr. **C8**
37 Cockburn St. **M16**
44 Cockburnhill Rd. **B8**
40 Cockit Hat Plantation **K11**
37 Cocklaw **C11**
19 Coffin La. **K15**
23 Coillesdene Av. **S16**
23 Coillesdene Cr. **S16**
23 Coillesdene Dr. **S16**
23 Coillesdene Gdns. **S16**
23 Coillesdene Gro. **S16**
23 Coillesdene Ho. **S16**
23 Coillesdene Ln. **T16**
23 Coillesdene Terr. **S16**
39 Colinton Castle **H12**
39 Colinton Dell **H12**
30 Colinton Gro. **J13**
30 Colinton Grove W. **J13**
40 Colinton Mains Cr. **K11**
40 Colinton Mains Dr. **J12**
40 Colinton Mains Gdns. **J12**
40 Colinton Mains Gro. **K12**
40 Colinton Mains Ln. **J12**
40 Colinton Mains Pk. **K12**
40 Colinton Mains Pl. **K12**
40 Colinton Mains Rd. **J12**
40 Colinton Mains Terr. **K12**
30 Colinton Rd. **J13**
40 Colinton Sch. (Primary) **J12**
7 College St. S. **M16**
7 College St. W. **M16**
College Wynd*=Cowgate
19 Collins Pl. **L17**
18 Coltbridge Av. **J16**
18 Coltbridge Gdns. **K16**
18 Coltbridge Terr. **J16**
18 Coltbridge Vale **K16**
18 Columba Av. **H17**
18 Columba Rd. **H17**
19 Colville Pl. **L17**
19 Comely Bk. **K17**
18 Comely Bank Av. **L17**
18 Comely Bank Cem. **K17**
19 Comely Bank Gro. **K17**
19 Comely Bank Pl. **L17**
19 Comely Bk. Pl. Mews **L17**
19 Comely Bank Rd. **K17**
19 Comely Bank Row **L17**
19 Comely Bank St. **K17**
19 Comely Bank Terr. **L17**
21 Comely Gr. Cr. **O17**
21 Comely Gr. Pl. **O17**
31 Comiston Dr. **K13**
31 Comiston Gdns. **L13**
14 Comiston Gro. **L12**
31 Comiston Pl. **L13**
41 Comiston Rise **L12**
41 Comiston Rd. **L12**
40 Comiston Sch. **K11**
41 Comiston Springs Av. **L12**
31 Comiston Terr. **L13**
41 Comiston Vw. **L12**
12 Commercial St. **N19**
12 Connaught Pl. **M19**
21 Considine Gdns. **P17**
21 Considine Terr. **P17**
12 Constitution Pl. **O19**
12 Constitution St. **O19**
Convening Ct.*=Dean Path
9 Corbiehill Av. **H18**
9 Corbiehill Cr. **G18**

9 Corbiehill Gdns. **H18**
9 Corbiehill Gro. **H18**
9 Corbiehill Pk. **H18**
9 Corbiehill Pl. **G18**
9 Corbiehill Rd. **G18**
9 Corbiehill Terr. **G18**
35 Corbieshot **R15**
30 Corn Exchange **J14**
13 Cornhill Terr. **O29**
9 Cornwall St. **L16**
12 Cornwallis Pl. **M17**
19 Coronation Walk **M15**
Corporation Bdgs.*=Sheriff Brae
31 Corrennie Dr. **L13**
31 Corrennie Gdns. **L13**
38 Corslet Cr. **E11**
38 Corslet Pl. **E11**
38 Corslet Rd. **E11**
16 Corstorphine Bank Av. **F16**
16 Corstorphine Bank Dr. **F16**
16 Corstorphine Bank Terr. **F16**
16 Corstorphine High St. **F15**
17 Corstorphine Hill **G17**
17 Corstorphine Hill Av. **G16**
16 Corstorphine Hill Cem. **F16**
17 Corstorphine Hill Cr. **G16**
17 Corstorphine Hill Gdns. **G16**
17 Corstorphine Hill Rd. **G16**
17 Corstorphine Hosp. **G15**
17 Corstorphine Ho. Av. **G15**
17 Corstorphine Ho. Terr. **G15**
17 Corstorphine Park **G15**
17 Corstorphine Park Gdns. **G15**
17 Corstorphine Rd. **G15**
16 Corstorphine Sch. **F15**
49 Cortleferry Dr. **T9**
Cortleferry Pk.*=Beech Grove Av.
Cortleferry Terr.*=Beech Grove Av.
12 Corunna Pl. **N19**
8 Cottage Gr. **E18**
40 Cottage Homes **H11**
25 Cottage La., *Muss.* **W15**
17 Cottage Pk. **H17**
7 County Hall **M16**
12 Couper St. **N19**
30 Cowan Rd. **K14**
7 Cowan's Cl. **N15**
50 Cowden Cr., *Dalk.* **V10**
50 Cowden Gr., *Dalk.* **V10**
50 Cowden Pk., *Dalk.* **V10**
50 Cowden Terr., *Dalk.* **V10**
50 Cowden Vw., *Dalk.* **V10**
7 Cowgate **M16**
20 Cowgatehead **M16**
25 Cowpits Ford Rd., *Muss.* **V14**
25 Cowpits Rd. **W13**
30 Coxfield **J14**
25 Craighall Terr., *Muss.* **W15**
Craig Ho.*=Thomas Clouston Clinic
35 Craig Pk. **S14**
17 Craigcrook Av. **G17**
17 Craigcrook Gro. **H17**
17 Craigcrook Pk. **H17**
18 Craigcrook Pl. **H17**
17 Craigcrook Rd. **G17**
18 Craigcrook Sq. **H17**
17 Craigcrook Terr. **H17**
22 Craigentinny Av. **Q17**
13 Craigentinny Av. N. **P18**
22 Craigentinny Cr. **Q17**
13 Craigentinny Golf Course **P18**
22 Craigentinny Gro. **Q17**
22 Craigentinny Pl. **Q17**
22 Craigentinny Rd. **P17**
22 Craigentinny Sch. **P17**
11 Craighall Av. **M19**

11 Craighall Bk. **M19**
11 Craighall Cr. **M19**
11 Craighall Gdns. **M19**
11 Craighall Rd. **M19**
11 Craighall Terr. **M19**
31 Craighill Gdns. **K13**
31 Craighouse Av. **K13**
31 Craighouse Gdns. **K13**
31 Craighouse Pk. **K13**
31 Craighouse Rd. **K13**
31 Craighouse Terr. **K13**
Craigievar Ct.*=Craigievar Wynd
16 Craigievar Sq. **E16**
16 Craigievar Wynd **E16**
31 Craiglea Dr. **K13**
31 Craiglea Pl. **K13**
18 Craigleith Av. N. **J16**
18 Craigleith Av. S. **J16**
18 Craigleith Bk. **J17**
18 Craigleith Cr. **J17**
18 Craigleith Dr. **J17**
18 Craigleith Gdns. **J17**
18 Craigleith Gro. **J17**
18 Craigleith Hill **J17**
18 Craigleith Hill Av. **J17**
18 Craigleith Hill Cr. **J17**
18 Craigleith Hill Gdns. **J17**
18 Craigleith Hill Gr. **J17**
18 Craigleith Hill Gro. **J17**
18 Craigleith Hill Ln. **J17**
18 Craigleith Hill Pk. **J17**
18 Craigleith Hill Row **J17**
18 Craigleith Rise **J16**
18 Craigleith Rd. **J17**
18 Craigleith Vw. **J16**
30 Craiglockhart Av. **J13**
30 Craiglockhart Bk. **J13**
30 Craiglockhart Cr. **J13**
30 Craiglockhart Dell **J13**
30 Craiglockhart Dell Rd. **J13**
30 Craiglockhart Dr. N. **J13**
30 Craiglockhart Dr. S. **J13**
30 Craiglockhart Gdns. **J13**
30 Craiglockhart Golf Course **K13**
30 Craiglockhart Gro. **J12**
30 Craiglockhart Ln. **J13**
30 Craiglockhart Pk. **J13**
30 Craiglockhart Pl. **J13**
30 Craiglockhart Qt. **J13**
30 Craiglockhart Rd. **J12**
30 Craiglockhart Rd. N. **J13**
31 Craiglockhart Sch. **K14**
30 Craiglockhart Sports Centre **J13**
30 Craiglockhart Terr. **K14**
30 Craiglockhart Vw. **J13**
34 Craigmillar Castle **P13**
34 Craigmillar Castle Av. **P14**
34 Craigmillar Castle Gdns. **P14**
34 Craigmillar Castle Gro. **P14**
34 Craigmillar Castle Ln. **Q14**
34 Craigmillar Castle Rd. **P14**
34· Craigmillar Castle Terr. **P14**
33 Craigmillar Ct. **P14**
33 Craigmillar Pk. (street) **N14**
34 Craigmillar Pk. **P14**
32 Craigmillar Park Golf Course **N13**
34 Craigmillar Sch. **Q14**
16 Craigmount Appr. **F16**
16 Craigmount Av. **F16**
16 Craigmount Av. N. **E17**
16 Craigmount Bk. **E17**
16 Craigmount Bank W. **E17**
16 Craigmount Brae **E17**
16 Craigmount Cr. **E16**
16 Craigmount Ct. **E17**
16 Craigmount Dr. **E16**
16 Craigmount Gdns. **E16**
16 Craigmount Gro. **E16**
16 Craigmount Gro. N. **E16**
16 Craigmount Hill **E17**

16 Craigmount Ln. **E16**
16 Craigmount Pk. **E16**
16 Craigmount Pl. **E16**
16 Craigmount Sch. **E16**
16 Craigmount Terr. **E16**
16 Craigmount Vw. **E16**
16 Craigmount Way **F17**
10 Craigmuir Sch. **J19**
43 Craigour Av. **Q12**
43 Craigour Cr. **Q12**
43 Craigour Dr. **Q12**
43 Craigour Gdns. **Q12**
43 Craigour Gr. **P12**
43 Craigour Gro. **Q12**
43 Craigour Ln. **Q12**
43 Craigour Pl. **P12**
43 Craigour Terr. **Q12**
10 Craigroyston Sch. **J18**
16 Craigs Av. **E15**
16 Craigs Bk. **E16**
16 Craigs Cr. **E16**
16 Craigs Dr. **E16**
16 Craigs Gdns. **E16**
16 Craigs Gro. **F15**
16 Craigs Ln. **F16**
16 Craigs Pk. **E16**
16 Craigs Rd. **E16**
49 Crame Terr. **T9**
8 Cramond Av. **E19**
8 Cramond Bk. **E19**
8 Cramond Brig Toll **D18**
8 Cramond Cr. **E19**
8 Cramond Gdns. **E19**
8 Cramond Glebe Gdns. **F19**
8 Cramond Glebe Rd. **E19**
8 Cramond Glebe Terr. **E19**
8 Cramond Gr. **E19**
8 Cramond Gro. **E19**
8 Cramond Pk. **E19**
8 Cramond Pl. **F19**
8 Cramond Regis **E18**
8 Cramond Rd. N. **F19**
9 Cramond Rd. S. **F19**
8 Cramond Sch. **E19**
8 Cramond Sch. Annexe **E19**
8 Cramond Terr. **E19**
8 Cramond Tower **F19**
8 Cramond Vale **E19**
7 Cranston St. **N16**
18 Crarae Av. **J16**
8 Craufordland **E18**
21 Crawford Bridge **O17**
33 Crawfurd Rd. **O14**
31 Crescent, The **L13**
Crescent, The*=Gorgie Rd.
18 Crest Hotel **J17**
10 Crewe Bank **K19**
10 Crewe Cr. **J19**
10 Crewe Gro. **K19**
10 Crewe Ln. **J19**
10 Crewe Path **J19**
10 Crewe Pl. **J19**
10 Crewe Rd. Gdns. **J19**
10 Crewe Rd. N. **J19**
10 Crewe Rd. S. **K18**
10 Crewe Rd. W. **J19**
10 Crewe Terr. **J19**
10 Crewe Toll **J18**
7 Crichton St. **M23**
12 Crighton Pl. **N18**
20 Croall Pl. **N17**
21 Croft-an-righ **N17**
50 Croft St., *Dalk.* **U10**
12 Cromwell Pl. **N19**
7 Crown Office Bldgs. **N17**
24 Crookston Rd., *Muss.* **W14**
44 Crosswood Av. **B8**
44 Crosswood Cr. **B8**
44 Crosswood Rd. **B8**
12 Crown Pl. **N18**
12 Crown St. **N18**
31 Cuddy La. **L14**
28 Cultins Rd. **E14**
19 Cumberland St. **M17**
19 Cumberland St. La., N.E. **M17**

19 Cumberland St. La., N.W. **M17**
19 Cumberland St. La., S.E. **M17**
19 Cumberland St. La., S.W. **M17**
32 Cumin Pl. **N15**
18 Cumlodden Av. **J16**
33 Cumnor Cr. **O13**
37 Currie High Sch. **D10**
45 Curriehill Castle Dr. **C10**
37 Curriehill Rd. **C12**
38 Curriehill Sch. **E10**
37 Curriehill Sta. **D11**
37 Currievale **D11**
37 Currievale Dr. **D10**
37 Currievale Pk. **D10**
37 Currievale Park Gr. **D10**
12 Custom Ho. **O19**

Dairsie Pl.*=Stanley Pl.
Daisy Terr.*=Merchiston Gro.
21 Dalgety Av. **O17**
21 Dalgety Rd. **O17**
21 Dalgety St. **O17**
50 Dalhousie Rd. **T9**
31 Dalhousie Terr. **L13**
32 Dalkeith Rd. **N15**
50 Dalkeith Sch., *Dalk.* **U10**
23 Dalkeith St. **S16**
36 Dalmahoy Country Club **A11**
44· Dalmahoy Cr. **C10**
36 Dalmahoy Golf Course **A11**
36 Dalmahoy Mains **A10**
36 Dalmahoy Rd. **A13**
12 Dalmeny Pk. **N18**
12 Dalmeny Rd. **M19**
12 Dalmeny St. **N18**
19 Dalry Cem. **K15**
19 Dalry Pl. **L16**
Dalry Rd. La.*=Dalry Rd.
19 Dalry Sch. **K15**
32 Dalrymple Cr. **N14**
24 Dalrymple Cr., *Muss.* **U15**
25 Dalrymple Ln., *Muss.* **V15**
47 Dalum Ct. **O8**
47 Dalum Dr. **O8**
47 Dalum Gr. **O8**
47 Dalum Ln. **O8**
Dalziel Pl.*=London Rd.
46 Damhead **M8**
19 Damside **L16**
51 Danderhall Cr. **R12**
51 Danderhall Sch. **R12**
19 Danube St. **L17**
Darling's Bdgs.*=Saunder's St.
6 Darnaway St. **L17**
11 Darnell Rd. **L19**
7 David Hume Tower **M15**
9 Davidson Gdns. **H18**
10 Davidson Pk. **K18**
10 Davidson Rd. **J18**
9 Davidson's Mains Pk. **G18**
9 Davidson's Mains Sch. **G18**
20 Davie St. **N16**
20 Deaconess Hosp. **N16**
19 Dean Bank La. **L17**
6 Dean Bridge **L17**
19 Dean Cem. **K17**
19 Dean Centre **K16**
19 Dean Park Cr. **L17**
19 Dean Park Mews **L17**
44 Dean Park Sch. **C8**
44 Dean Park School Annexe **C9**
19 Dean Park St. **L17**
19 Dean Path **K17**

Dean Path Bdgs.*=Dean Path
19 Dean St. **L17**
19 Dean Terr. **L17**
21 Deanery Cl. **P17**
19 Deanhaugh St. **L17**
44 Deanpark Av. **C9**
45 Deanpark Bk. **C9**
45 Deanpark Brae **C9**
44 Deanpark Ct. **B9**
45 Deanpark Cr. **C9**
45 Deanpark Gdns. **C9**
45 Deanpark Gro. **C9**
44 Deanpark Pl. **C9**
44 Deanpark Sq. **C9**
16 Dechmont Rd. **E16**
30 Delhaig **J14**
39 Dell Rd. **H12**
25 Delta Pl., *Muss.* **V14**
11 Denham Green Av. **L19**
11· Denham Green Pl. **L30**
11 Denham Green Terr. **L19**
11 Derby St. **M19**
19 Devon Pl. **K16**
6 Dewar Pl. **L16**
6 Dewar Pl. La. **L16**
32 Dick Pl. **M14**
12 Dickson St. **N18**
Dickson's Cl.*=High St.
Dickson's Ct.*=Bristo St.
33 Dinmont Dr. **O13**
Distillery La.*=Dalry Rd.
49 Dobbie's Rd. **R8**
16 Dochart Dr. **F17**
12 Dock Pl. **N19**
12 Dock St. **N19**
37 Dolphin Av. **D10**
37 Dolphin Gdns. E. **D10**
37 Dolphin Gdns. W. **D10**
37 Dolphin Rd. **D10**
31 Dominion Cinema **L14**
19 Donaldson's Sch. (for the deaf) **K16**
19 Dorset Pl. **L15**
25 Double Dykes, *Muss.* **V14**
33 Double Hedges Pk. **O13**
33 Double Hedges Rd. **O13**
49 Douglas Cr. **R8**
19 Douglas Cr. **K16**
19 Douglas Gdns. **K16**
19 Douglas Gdns. Mews **K16**
19 Douglas Terr. **L16**
6 Doune Terr. **L17**
29 Dovecot Gro. **H13**
29 Dovecot Ln. **H13**
29 Dovecot Pk. (st.) **H13**
29 Dovecot Pk. **H13**
29 Dovecot Rd. **F15**
8 Dowie's Mill La. **D18**
19 Downfield Pl. **K15**
17 Downie Gro. **G15**
25 Downie Pl., *Muss.* **V15**
17 Downie Terr. **G15**
40 Dreghorn Av. **K11**
40 Dreghorn Dr. **K11**
40 Dreghorn Gdns. **K11**
40 Dreghorn Gro. **K11**
40 Dreghorn Link **K11**
39 Dreghorn Ln. **H11**
40 Dreghorn Pk. **J11**
40 Dreghorn Pl. **K11**
43 Drum Av. **Q11**
16 Drum Brae Av. **F18**
16 Drum Brae Cr. **F17**
16 Drum Brae Dr. **F28**
16 Drum Brae Gdns. **F16**
16 Drum Brae Gro. **F17**
16 Drum Brae Neuk **F16**
16 Drum Brae N. **E17**
16 Drum Brae Pk. (st.) **F19**
16 Drum Brae Pk. **F17**
Drum Brae Park Appr.*=Drum Brae Pk.
16 Drum Brae Pl. **F16**
16 Drum Brae S. **F16**
16 Drum Brae Terr. **F17**

16 Drum Brae Walk **F17**
43 Drum Cotts. **Q11**
43 Drum Cr. **Q11**
51 Drum Farm **R11**
 Drum Park Yard*=Albion Rd.
43 Drum Pl. **Q11**
43 Drum St. **Q11**
21 Drum Terr. **O17**
51 Drum View Av. **R12**
16 Drumbrae Sch. **F16**
6 Drumdryan St. **M15**
6 Drummond Pl. **M17**
20 Drummond Sch. **M17**
7 Drummond St. **N16**
6 Drumsheugh Gdns. **L16**
 Drumsheugh Pl*=Queensferry St.
47 Dryden Av. **O8**
47 Dryden Cr. **O8**
12 Dryden Gdns. **N18**
32 Dryden Pl. **N15**
12 Dryden St. **N18**
12 Dryden Terr. **N18**
47 Dryden Terr. **O8**
47 Dryden Vw. **O8**
18 Drylaw Av. **J17**
18 Drylaw Cr. **H17**
18 Drylaw Gdns. **H18**
18 Drylaw Gr. **H17**
18 Drylaw Gro. **H17**
10 Drylaw Ho. **H18**
10 Drylaw Ho. Gdns. **H18**
10 Drylaw Ho. Padd. **H18**
10 Drylaw Sch. **J18**
16 Duart Cr. **F17**
6 Dublin Meuse **M17**
7 Dublin St. **M17**
7 Dublin St. La. **M17**
22 Duddingston Av. **Q15**
22 Duddingston Cr. **R15**
22 Duddingston Gdns. N. **Q16**
22 Duddingston Gdns. S. **Q15**
22 Duddingston Golf Course **Q15**
22 Duddingston Gro. E. **Q16**
22 Duddingston Gro. W. **Q15**
22 Duddingston Ln. **Q15**
 Duddingston Mains Cotts.*=Milton Rd.
22 Duddingston Mills Cotts. **Q16**
22 Duddingston Pk. **R16**
34 Duddingston Park S. **R15**
22 Duddingston Rise **Q15**
22 Duddingston Rd. **Q16**
22 Duddingston Row **Q15**
22 Duddingston Sch. **Q16**
22 Duddingston Sq. E. **Q16**
22 Duddingston Sq. W. **Q16**
22 Duddingston Vw. **Q15**
21 Duddingston Village **P15**
 Duddingston Yards*=Duddingston Pk. S.
12 Dudley Av. **M19**
12 Dudley Av. S. **N19**
12 Dudley Bk. **M19**
12 Dudley Cr. **M19**
12 Dudley Gdns. **M19**
12 Dudley Gro. **M19**
12 Dudley Terr. **M19**
19 Duff St. **K15**
19 Duff St. La. **K15**
12 Duke Pl. **O18**
12 Duke St. **O18**
50 Duke St., *Dalk.* **U10**
21 Duke's Walk **O17**
29 Dumbiedykes Rd. **N16**
29 Dumbryden Dr. **G13**
29 Dumbryden Gdns. **G13**
29 Dumbryden Gro. **G13**
29 Dumbryden Rd. **G13**
29 Dumbryden Sch. **G13**
32 Dun-Ard Gdns. **M14**
6 Dunbar St. **L15**

12 Duncan Pl. **O18**
32 Duncan St. **N14**
29 Duncans Gait **H13**
50 Dundas Cr. **T9**
49 Dundas Pk. **S8**
50 Dundas Rd. **T9**
49 Dundas St. **R8**
20 Dundas St. **M17**
19 Dundee St. **K15**
19 Dundee Terr. **K15**
20 Dundonald St. **M17**
33 Dundrennan Cotts. **P13**
33 Dunedin Sch. **O13**
33 Dunedin Sch. **O13**
12 Dunedin St. **M18**
8 Dunfermline Coll. of Physical Education **F19**
 Dunlop's Ct.*=Grassmarket
 Dunollie Ct.*=Craigievar Wynd
19 Dunrobin Pl. **L17**
16 Dunsmuir Ct. **F15**
28 Dunsyre Ho. **F13**
8 Dunvegan Ct. **E18**
16 Durar Dr. **F17**
22 Durham Av. **Q16**
22 Durham Dr. **R15**
22 Durham Gdns. N. **R16**
22 Durham Gdns. S. **R15**
22 Durham Gro. **R16**
 Durham Pl.*=Dundas St.
22 Durham Pl. E. **R16**
22 Durham Pl. W. **Q16**
22 Durham Pl. La. **R16**
22 Durham Rd. **R16**
22 Durham Rd. S. **R15**
22 Durham Sq. **R16**
22 Durham Terr. **Q16**
33 Durward Gro. **O13**

6 Earl Grey St. **L16**
11 Earl Haig Gdns. **L19**
29 Earl Haig Homes **H14**
21 Earlston Pl. **O17**
7 East Adam St. **N16**
9 East Barnton Av. **G18**
9 East Barnton Gdns. **G18**
22 East Brighton Cr. **R16**
 East Broughton Pl.*=Broughton Pl.
41 East Caiystane Pl. **L11**
41 East Caiystane Rd. **L11**
31 East Castle Rd. **L15**
32 East Champanyie **N14**
33 East Clapperfield **O13**
12 East Claremont St. **M17**
18 East Ct. **J17**
8 East Craigie **D19**
16 East Craigs **E16**
16 East Craigs Fm. **E16**
16 East Craigs Sch. **E16**
26 East Croft **A13**
12 East Cromwell St. **N19**
7 East Crosscauseway **N15**
43 East Farm of Gilmerton **Q11**
11 East Fettes Av. **K18**
6 East Fountainbridge **L16**
44 East Hannahfield **B9**
36 East Hatton Mains **A12**
28 East Hermiston **E13**
13 East Hermitage Pl. **O18**
11 East Lillypot **L19**
20 East London St. **M17**
7 East Market St. **N16**
32 East Mayfield **N14**
32 East Newington Pl. **N15**
21 East Norton Pl. **N17**
20 East Parkside **N15**
10 East Pilton Pk. **K19**
20 East Preston St. **N15**
 East Preston St. La.*=East Preston St.
7 East Princes St. Gdns. **M16**
13 East Restalrig Terr. **O18**

32 East Savile Rd. **N14**
20 East Sciennes St. **N15**
20 East Silvermills La. **L17**
33 East Suffolk Rd. **O14**
22 East Telferton **Q17**
11 East Trinity Rd. **L19**
22 East Way, The **Q16**
10 East Werberside **K18**
18 Easter Belmont Rd. **H16**
30 Easter Craiglockhart Hill **K13**
38 Easter Currie Ct. **E10**
38 Easter Currie Cr. **E11**
38 Easter Currie Pl. **E11**
38 Easter Currie Terr. **E10**
10 Easter Drylaw Av. **J18**
10 Easter Drylaw Bk. **J18**
10 Easter Drylaw Dr. **J18**
10 Easter Drylaw Gdns. **J18**
10 Easter Drylaw Gro. **J18**
10 Easter Drylaw Ln. **J18**
10 Easter Drylaw Pl. **J18**
10 Easter Drylaw Vw. **J18**
10 Easter Drylaw Way **J18**
40 Easter Haugh **K12**
26 Easter Norton **B15**
9 Easter Park Dr. **G18**
21 Easter Rd. **N17**
12 Eastern Cem. **O18**
13 Eastern General Hosp. **P18**
31 Easter Steil **K13**
11 Easter Warriston **M18**
11 Easter Warriston **M18**
23 Eastfield **T16**
23 Eastfield Gdns. **T16**
14 Eastfield Rd. **B15**
24 Eastfield Pl. **E16**
50 Easthouses Rd., *Dalk.* **V9**
31 Eden La. **L14**
 Eden Terr.*=Newbattle Terr.
25 Edenhall Bk., *Muss.* **W15**
25 Edenhall Cr., *Muss.* **W15**
25 Edenhall Hospital, *Muss.* **W14**
25 Edenhall Rd., *Muss.* **W15**
48 Edgefield **P9**
47 Edgefield Industrial Estate **P9**
47 Edgefield Pl. **P8**
47 Edgefield Rd. **P9**
48 Edgefield Toll **P9**
21 Edina Pl. **O17**
20 Edina St. **N17**
19 Edinburgh Acad. **L17**
11 Edinburgh Acad. New Field **K18**
11 Edinburgh Acad. (Primary) **L18**
19 Edinburgh Acad. Sports Ground **L17**
14 Edinburgh Airport **A16**
51 Edinburgh Butterfly Fm. **S10**
6 Edinburgh Coll. of Art **M16**
7 Edinburgh Dental Hosp. & Sch. **M16**
14 Edinburgh Exhibition and Trade Centre **A16**
50 Edinburgh Rd., *Dalk.* **U10**
50 Edinburgh Rd., Eskbank **T9**
24 Edinburgh Rd., *Muss.* **T16**
32 Edinburgh Sch. of Agriculture **N13**
43 Edinburgh Southern Harriers **Q12**
33 Edinburgh University Sports Grd. **P14**
33 Edinburgh University Theatre **M15**
51 Edmonstone Av. **R12**
51 Edmonstone Dr. **R12**
51 Edmonstone Rd. **R12**
51 Edmonstone Terr. **R12**
30 Education Committee Athletic Grd. **J14**

19 Eglinton Cr. **K16**
19 Eglinton St. **K16**
31 Egypt Mews **M14**
11 Eildon St. **M18**
11 Eildon Terr. **L18**
12 Elbe St. **O19**
23 Elcho Terr. **S16**
7 Elder St. **M17**
7 Elder St. E. **M17**
49 Eldindean Pl. **R8**
49 Eldindean Rd. **R8**
49 Eldindean Terr. **R8**
22 Electra Pl. **R17**
11 Elgin Pl. **K16**
20 Elgin Terr. **N17**
12 Elizafield **N18**
 Elizafield*=Newhaven Rd.
33 Ellangowan Terr. **P13**
43 Ellen's Glen **P12**
43 Ellen's Glen Rd. **P12**
18 Ellersly Ho. Hotel **J16**
18 Ellersly Rd. **J16**
40 Elliot Gdns. **J12**
40 Elliot Pk. **J12**
40 Elliot Pl. **J12**
40 Elliot Rd. **J12**
12 Elliot St. **N17**
13 Elm Pl. **O18**
20 Elm Row **N17**
49 Elm Row **R9**
50 Elmfield Pk., *Dalk.* **U10**
50 Elmfield Rd., *Dalk.* **U10**
13 Elmwood Terr. **O18**
30 Eltringham Gdns. **J14**
30 Eltringham Gro. **J14**
30 Eltringham Terr. **J14**
47 Engine Rd. **P8**
19 Episcopal Theological Coll. **K16**
 Erskine Pl.*=Shandwick Pl.
32 Esdaile **M14**
50 Esk Pl., *Dalk.* **T10**
49 Eskbank Rd. **S8**
50 Eskbank Rd., *Dalk.* **T9**
50 Eskbank Terr., *Dalk.* **T9**
49 Eskdale Ct. **R8**
48 Eskdale Dr. **R8**
24 Eskdale Mews, *Muss.* **V15**
49 Eskdale Terr. **R8**
48 Eskgrove **Q8**
24 Eskmill Villas, *Muss.* **U15**
 Eskside Court*=Ironmills Road
25 Eskside E., *Muss.* **V15**
24 Eskside W., *Muss.* **V15**
24 Eskview Av., *Muss.* **U15**
24 Eskview Cr., *Muss.* **U15**
50 Eskview Gr., *Dalk.* **T10**
24 Eskview Gr., *Muss.* **U15**
50 Eskview Pl. **T10**
24 Eskview Terr., *Muss.* **U15**
50 Eskview Villas, *Muss.* **T9**
8 Esplanade **F20**
23 Esplanade Terr. **S16**
16 Essendean Pl. **F17**
16 Essendean Terr. **F17**
8 Essex Brae **E18**
8 Essex Pk. **E18**
8 Essex Rd. **E18**
32 Esslemont Rd. **N13**
18 Esso Motor Hotel **J17**
31 Ethel Terr. **L13**
6 Eton Terr. **L17**
31 Ettrick Gro. **L15**
31 Ettrick Rd. **K14**
19 Ettrickdale Pl. **L17**
32 Eva Pl. **N13**
49 Evans Gdns. **S8**
19 Eyre Cr. **M17**
19 Eyre Pl. **M17**
19 Eyre Terr. **M17**

8 Fair-a-Far **E19**
8 Fair-a-Far Cotts. **E19**

33 Fairford Gdns. **O13**
41 Fairmile Av. **L11**
41 Fairmile Nursing Home **M11**
41 Fairmilehead **L11**
41 Fairmilehead Pk. **L11**
14 Fairview Rd. **A16**
24 Fairways **U14**
24 Fairways, *Muss.* **U15**
43 Fala Ct. **O11**
31 Falcon Av. **L14**
31 Falcon Ct. **L14**
31 Falcon Gdns. **L14**
31 Falcon Rd. **L14**
31 Falcon Rd. W. **L14**
17 Falkland Gdns. **G17**
22 Farrer Gro. **Q17**
22 Farrer Terr. **Q17**
16 Fauldburn **E17**
16 Fauldburn Pk. **E17**
16 Featherhall Av. **F15**
16 Featherhall Cr. N. **F15**
16 Featherhall Cr. S. **F15**
16 Featherhall Gro. **F15**
16 Featherhall Pl. **F15**
16 Featherhall Rd. **F15**
16 Featherhall Terr. **F15**
43 Ferniehill Av. **Q11**
43 Ferniehill Dr. **Q11**
43 Ferniehill Gdns. **Q12**
43 Ferniehill Gro. **Q12**
43 Ferniehill Pl. **Q11**
43 Ferniehill Rd. **Q11**
43 Ferniehill Sq. **Q11**
43 Ferniehill St. **Q12**
43 Ferniehill Terr. **Q11**
43 Ferniehill Way **Q12**
25 Fernielaw, *Muss.* **V13**
39 Fernielaw Av. **H11**
43 Fernieside Av. **Q12**
43 Fernieside Cr. **Q12**
43 Fernieside Dr. **Q12**
43 Fernieside Gdns. **Q12**
43 Fernieside Gro. **Q12**
43 Fernieside Sch. **Q12**
10 Ferry Rd. **H18**
10 Ferry Rd. Av. **J18**
10 Ferry Rd. Dr. **J19**
10 Ferry Rd. Gdns. **J18**
10 Ferry Rd. Gro. **J18**
10 Ferry Rd. Pl. **J18**
11 Ferryfield **K19**
10 Ferryhill Sch. **J18**
7 Festival Fringe Office **M16**
7 Festival Office **M16**
6 Festival Sq. **L16**
19 Fettes Av. **K17**
10 Fettes Coll. **K18**
11 Fettes Rise **K18**
20 Fettes Row **M28**
10 Fettes Sch. **K18**
9 Fidra Ct. **H19**
23 Figgate Bk. **R17**
22 Figgate Burn Pk. **Q16**
22 Figgate La. **R17**
22 Figgate St. **R17**
22 Fillyside Av. **Q17**
13 Fillyside Rd. **Q18**
22 Fillyside Terr. **Q18**
6 Filmhouse **L16**
32 Findhorn Pl. **N14**
13 Findlay Av. **P18**
13 Findlay Cotts. **P18**
13 Findlay Gdns. **P18**
13 Findlay Gro. **P18**
13 Findlay Medway **P18**
32 Fingal Pl. **M15**
13 Fingzies Pl. **O18**
Finlaggan Ct.*=Craigievar Wynd
40 Firrhill Cr. **K12**
40 Firrhill Dr. **K12**
40 Firrhill Ln. **K12**
40 Firrhill Sch. **J12**
37 First Gait **D12**
12 Fish Market **M20**
24 Fisherrow Harbour, *Muss.* **U16**

25 Fisherrow Links, *Muss.* **V16**
25 Fisherrow Sands, *Muss.* **V16**
24 Fishers Wynd, *Muss.* **U15**
12 Fishmarket Sq. **M20**
22 Fishwives' Causeway **Q17**
Fleshmarket Cl.*=High St.
19 Flora Stevenson Sch. **K17**
31 Forbes Rd. **L15**
7 Forbes St. **N15**
30 Fords Rd. **H14**
17 Forestry Commission **G15**
6 Forres St. **L17**
7 Forrest Hill **M16**
7 Forrest Rd. **M16**
29 Forrester Park Av. **F14**
29 Forrester Park Dr. **F14**
28 Forrester Park Gdns. **F14**
29 Forrester Park Gr. **G14**
29 Forrester Park Gro. **F14**
29 Forrester Park Ln. **F14**
16 Forrester Rd. **F16**
28 Forrester Sch. **F14**
12 Fort Ho. **N19**
12 Fort Sch. **N19**
43 Forteviot Ho. **P12**
32 Forteviot Sch. **M14**
7 Forth St. **M17**
38 Forth View Av. **D10**
37 Forth View Cr. (Currie) **D10**
51 Forth View Cr. (Danderhall) **R12**
38 Forth View Rd. **D10**
18 Forthview Rd. **J17**
18 Forthview Terr. **H17**
39 Foulis Cr. **F11**
48 Foundry La. **P9**
6 Fountainbridge **L15**
47 Fountain Pl. **P8**
32 Fountainhall Rd. **N14**
37 Fourth Gait **D12**
48 Fowler Sq. **P8**
31 Fowler Terr. **K15**
17 Fox Covert Av. **G17**
17 Fox Covert Gro. **G17**
17 Fox Covert Sch. **G16**
41 Fox Spring Cr. **L12**
41 Fox Spring Rise **L12**
11 Fraser Av. **L19**
11 Fraser Cr. **L19**
11 Fraser Gdns. **L19**
11 Fraser Gro. **L19**
Fraser Homes*=Spylaw Bank Rd.
6 Frederick St. **M17**
20 Free Church Coll. **M16**
6 Freemasons' Hall **M16**
41 Frogston Av. **L11**
41 Frogston Gdns. **L11**
41 Frogston Gro. **M11**
42 Frogston Rd. E. **N10**
41 Frogston Rd. W. **L11**
41 Frogston Terr. **M11**
30 Fruit Market **J14**
7 Fruit Market Gall. **M16**

Gabriel's Rd.*=West Register St.
41 Galachlaw Shot **M11**
41 Galachlawside **M11**
40 Gallolee, The **J11**
25 Galt Av., *Muss.* **X15**
25 Galt Cr., *Muss.* **X15**
8 Gamekeeper's Ln. **E19**
8 Gamekeeper's Pk. **E18**
8 Gamekeeper's Rd. **E19**
8 Garden Terr. **G18**
17 Gardiner Gro. **H17**
17 Gardiner Rd. **H17**
17 Gardiner Terr. **H17**
Gardner St.*=Lower London Rd.
6 Gardner's Cr. **L16**
18 Garscube Terr. **J16**
42 Garvald Ct. **O11**

20 Gayfield Pl. **N17**
20 Gayfield Pl. La. **N17**
20 Gayfield Sq. **N17**
20 Gayfield St. **N17**
47 Gaynor Av. **O8**
7 General Post Office **M16**
General's Entry*=Bristo St.
47 George Av. **O8**
7 George Cr. **P9**
47 George Dr. **O8**
7 George IV Bridge **M16**
7 George Heriot's Sch. **M16**
11 George Heriot's Sports Grd. **L18**
6 George Hotel **M17**
12 George Pl. **N18**
7 George Sq. **M15**
7 George Sq. La. **M15**
6 George St. **L16**
47 George Terr. **O8**
31 George Watson's Coll. **L14**
31 George Watson's Coll. Recreation Grd. **K14**
Gibb's Entry*=Simon Sq.
50 Gibraltar Ct., *Dalk.* **U10**
50 Gibraltar Gdns., *Dalk.* **U10**
50 Gibraltar Rd., *Dalk.* **U10**
50 Gibraltar Terr., *Dalk.* **U10**
12 Gibson Dr., *Dalk.* **V10**
32 Gibson St. **N18**
19 Gibson Terr. **L15**
7 Gifford Pk. **N15**
23 Gilbertstoun **S15**
23 Gilbertstoun Pl. **S15**
Gilchrist's Entry*=Leith St.
Gilchrist's La.*=Greenside Row
10 Giles St. **N19**
19 Gillespie Cr. **L15**
19 Gillespie Pl. **L15**
39 Gillespie Rd. **G11**
19 Gillespie St. **L15**
31 Gillsland Pk. **K14**
31 Gillsland Rd. **K14**
43 Gilmerton Dykes Av. **P11**
43 Gilmerton Dykes Cr. **P11**
43 Gilmerton Dykes Dr. **P11**
43 Gilmerton Dykes Gdns. **P11**
43 Gilmerton Dykes Gro. **P11**
43 Gilmerton Dykes Ln. **P11**
43 Gilmerton Dykes Pl. **P11**
43 Gilmerton Dykes Rd. **P10**
43 Gilmerton Dykes St. **P11**
43 Gilmerton Dykes Terr. **P11**
43 Gilmerton Dykes Vw. **P11**
43 Gilmerton Pk. **Q11**
33 Gilmerton Rd. **O13**
50 Gilmerton Rd. **T9**
43 Gilmerton Sch. **P11**
43 Gilmerton Station Rd. **Q10**
19 Gilmore Pk. **L15**
19 Gilmore Pl. **L15**
19 Gilmore Pl. La. **L15**
Gilmour's Entry*=Gilmour St.
32 Gilmour Rd. **N14**
7 Gilmour St. **N16**
13 Gladstone Pl. **O18**
19 Gladstone Terr. **N15**
Glanville Pl.*=Kerr St.
14 Glasgow Rd. **A15**
17 Glebe Gdns. **G15**
17 Glebe Gro. **F15**
Glebe Pl.*=High St.
48 Glebe Pl. **Q9**
17 Glebe Rd. **F15**
50 Glebe St., *Dalk.* **U10**
17 Glebe Terr. **F15**
8 Glebe, The **E19**
32 Glen St. **M15**
33 Glenallan Dr. **O13**
33 Glenallan Ln. **O13**
29 Glenalmond Ct. **F13**
19 Glencairn Cr. **K16**

44 Glenbrook **A8**
44 Glenbrook Ho. **A8**
44 Glenbrook Rd. **A8**
18 Glendevon Av. **H15**
18 Glendevon Gdns. **H15**
18 Glendevon Gro. **H15**
18 Glendevon Park **H15**
18 Glendevon Pl. **H15**
18 Glendevon Rd. **H15**
18 Glendevon Terr. **H15**
42 Glendinning Cr. **O12**
50 Glenesk Cr., *Dalk.* **T9**
6 Glenfinlas St. **L16**
19 Glengyle Terr. **L15**
32 Glenisla Gdns. **M14**
Glenisla Gdns. La.*=Glenisla Gdns.
30 Glenlea Cotts. **J14**
21 Glenlee Av. **P16**
21 Glenlee Gdns. **P16**
30 Glenlockhart Bk. **J13**
30 Glenlockhart Rd. **J13**
30 Glenlockhart Valley **J13**
19 Glenogle Ho. **L17**
19 Glenogle Pl. **L17**
19 Glenogle Rd. **L17**
19 Glenogle Terr. **L18**
Glenorchy Pl.*=Greenside Row
32 Glenorchy Terr. **N14**
44 Glenpark **A9**
18 Glenure Loan **F17**
33 Glenvarloch Cr. **O12**
6 Gloucester La. **L17**
6 Gloucester Pl. **L17**
Gloucester Sq.*=Gloucester La.
6 Gloucester St. **L17**
7 Goff Av. **Q17**
14 Gogar Mains **C16**
15 Gogar Mains Farm Rd. **C16**
26 Gogar Mount **B15**
27 Gogar Park Curling Club **D15**
27 Gogar Station Rd. **D13**
27 Gogarbank **D14**
27 Gogarburn Fm. **D14**
27 Gogarburn Hosp. **C15**
28 Gogarloch Rd. **E15**
15 Gogarside Roundabout **D15**
11 Goldenacre Terr. **L18**
47 Goldie Terr. **O8**
9 Golf Course Rd. **R8**
17 Gordon Ln. **G16**
17 Gordon Rd. **G16**
12 Gordon St. **O18**
33 Gordon Terr. **O13**
Gorgie Cotts.*=Gorgie Rd.
30 Gorgie Rd. **H14**
7 Gosford Pl. **M19**
11 Goodtrees **B8**
25 Goose Green Av., *Muss.* **V16**
25 Goose Green Cr., *Muss.* **V16**
25 Goose Green Pl., *Muss.* **V16**
25 Goose Green Rd., *Muss.* **V16**
36 Gowanhill **C11**
36 Gowanhill Rd. **C11**
20 G.P.O. Sorting Office **N17**
20 Gracefield Ct.*=Fishers Wynd
42 Gracemount Av. **O12**
43 Gracemount Dr. **O11**
43 Gracemount Pk. **P11**
42 Gracemount Pl. **O11**
43 Gracemount Rd. **O11**
43 Gracemount Sch. **O11**
43 Gracemount Sch. (Secondary) **P11**
42 Gracemount Sq. **O12**
12 Graham St. **N19**
12 Grampian Ho. **N19**
32 Granby Rd. **N14**

11 Grandfield **M19**
11 Grandville **M19**
32 Grange Cem. **M14**
  Grange
    Ct.*=Causewayside
32 Grange Cr. **M14**
19 Grange Cricket Grd. **L17**
32 Grange Ln. **M14**
32 Grange Loan Gdns. **M14**
32 Grange Rd. **M15**
32 Grange Terr. **M14**
39 Grant Av. **H11**
10 Granton Cr. **K19**
11 Granton Cr. Pk. **K19**
11 Granton Gdns. **K19**
10 Granton Gro. **K19**
10 Granton Medway **K19**
10 Granton Park Av. **K20**
11 Granton Pl. **K19**
11 Granton Rd. **L19**
10 Granton Sch. **K19**
11 Granton Sq. **K20**
11 Granton Terr. **K19**
11 Granton Vw. **K19**
32 Grantully Pl. **N14**
31 Granville Terr. **L15**
6 Grassmarket **M16**
31 Gray's Loan **K14**
30 Graysmill Sch. **H13**
22 Great Cannon Bk. **R17**
12 Great Junction St. **N19**
6 Great King St. **M17**
12 Great Michael Rise **M19**
  Great Michael Sq.*=Main
  St.
6 Great Stuart St. **L16**
20 Green St. **M17**
9 Green, The **G18**
45 Green, The **C8**
39 Green Way, The **G12**
31 Greenbank Av. **L13**
31 Greenbank Cr. **K12**
31 Greenbank Dr. **K13**
31 Greenbank Gdns. **K12**
41 Greenbank Gro. **K12**
31 Greenbank La. **K13**
31 Greenbank Ln. **K12**
31 Greenbank Pk. **K12**
31 Greenbank Pl. **L13**
41 Greenbank Rise **K12**
41 Greenbank Rd. **K12**
41 Greenbank Row **K12**
31 Greenbank Terr. **L13**
34 Greendykes Av. **Q14**
34 Greendykes Dr. **Q14**
34 Greendykes Gdns. **Q14**
34 Greendykes Ho. **Q14**
34 Greendykes Ln. **Q14**
34 Greendykes Rd. **Q14**
34 Greendykes Sch. **Q14**
34 Greendykes Terr. **Q14**
43 Greenend Dr. **P12**
43 Greenend Gdns. **P12**
43 Greenend Gro. **P12**
45 Greenfield Cr. **C8**
45 Greenfield Rd. **C8**
31 Greenhill Gdns. **L15**
31 Greenhill Pk. **L14**
31 Greenhill Pl. **L14**
31 Greenhill Terr. **L15**
40 Greenlaw Hedge **K12**
40 Greenlaw Rig **K12**
33 Greenmantle Ln. **O12**
  Greenside Ct.*=Greenside
  Row
7 Greenside La. **N17**
7 Greenside Pl. **N17**
18 Greenwood **J16**
7 Greenside Row **N17**
7 Greyfriars Kirk **M16**
  Greyfriars
  Pl.*=Candlemaker Row
11 Grierson Av. **L19**
11 Grierson Cr. **L19**
11 Grierson Gdns. **L19**
11 Grierson Rd. **K19**
11 Grierson Sq. **L19**
11 Grierson Villas **L19**

10 Grigor Av. **J18**
10 Grigor Dr. **J18**
10 Grigor Gdns. **J19**
10 Grigor Terr. **J18**
6 Grindlay St. **L16**
6 Grindlay St. Ct. **L16**
18 Groathill Av. **J17**
18 Groathill Gdns. E. **J17**
18 Groathill Gdns. W. **J17**
18 Groathill Rd. N. **J18**
18 Groathill Rd. S. **J17**
19 Grosvenor Cr. **K16**
19 Grosvenor Gdns. **K16**
19 Grosvenor St. **L16**
38 Grove Pl. **F11**
6 Grove St. **L16**
25 Grove St., *Muss.* **V15**
25 Grove, The, *Muss.* **W15**
  Grove Terr.*=Grove St.
18 Guardianswood **J16**
7 Gullan's Cl. **N16**
9 Gunnet Ct. **H19**
7 Guthrie St. **M16**
16 Gyle Park, The **E15**
16 Gyle Park Gdns. **E15**
16 Gylemuir Rd. **F15**
16 Gylemuir Sch. **F15**
10 Gypsy Brae **J19**

20 Haddington Pl. **N17**
  Haddington's
  Entry*=Reid's Cl.
  Haddon Ct.*=Howden St.
39 Hailes Appr. **H12**
39 Hailes Av. **H12**
39 Hailes Bk. **H12**
39 Hailes Cr. **H12**
39 Hailes Gdns. **G12**
39 Hailes Gro. **H12**
39 Hailes Pk. (street) **G12**
29 Hailes Pk. **G13**
  Hailes Quarry
  Cott.*=Murrayburn Rd.
19 Hailes St. **L15**
39 Hailes Terr. **H12**
29 Hailesland Gdns. **G13**
29 Hailesland Gro. **G13**
29 Hailesland Pk. **G13**
29 Hailesland Pl. **G13**
39 Hailesland Rd. **G13**
39 Hailesland Sch. **G12**
40 Hainburn Pk. **K11**
17 Hall Terr. **G15**
33 Hallhead Rd **N13**
12 Halmyre St. **N18**
  Hamburgh Pl.*=Portland
  St.
22 Hamilton Dr. **Q16**
22 Hamilton Dr. W. **Q16**
22 Hamilton Gdns. **Q16**
22 Hamilton Gro. **Q16**
22 Hamilton Park **Q16**
19 Hamilton Pl. **L17**
22 Hamilton Terr. **R16**
12 Hamilton Wynd **N19**
  Hampton Pl.*=West
  Catherine Pl.
18 Hampton Terr. **K16**
6 Hanover St. **M17**
22 Harbour Pl. **R17**
24 Harbour Rd., *Muss.* **U15**
22 Harbour Rd. **R17**
31 Harden Pl. **K15**
20 Hardwell Cl. **N15**
39 Harelaw Rd. **H11**
34 Harewood Cr. **Q14**
34 Harewood Dr. **Q14**
34 Harewood Rd. **Q14**
45 Harlaw **D8**
45 Harlaw March **C8**
45 Harlaw Rd. **C8**
45 Harmeny **C8**
30 Harrison Gdns. **K14**
31 Harrison La. **K15**
31 Harrison Pk. **K15**
30 Harrison Pl. **K14**
31 Harrison Rd. **K15**

7 Hart St. **M17**
  Hart St. La.*=Hart St.
31 Hartington Gdns. **L15**
31 Hartington Pl. **L15**
32 Hatton Pl. **M15**
24 Haugh Pk., *Muss.* **U15**
19 Haugh St. **L17**
42 Hawkhead Cr. **O12**
42 Hawkhead Gro. **O12**
12 Hawkhill Av. **O18**
13 Hawkhill Ct. **O18**
  Hawkhill Villas*=Lochend
  Rd.
  Hawthorne Bdgs.*=Belford
  Rd.
47 Hawthorn Gdns. **O9**
  Hawthorn
  Terr.*=Hawthornbank
  La.
19 Hawthornbank La. **L16**
12 Hawthornbank Pl. **N19**
12 Hawthornbank Terr. **N19**
49 Hawthornden Av. **R8**
49 Hawthornden Gdns. **R8**
12 Hawthornden Pl. **N18**
43 Hawthorne Pl. **Q11**
12 Hawthornvale **M19**
34 Hay Av. **Q14**
34 Hay Dr. **R14**
34 Hay Pl. **Q14**
34 Hay Rd. **Q14**
34 Hay Terr. **Q14**
19 Haymarket **L16**
19 Haymarket Sta. **L16**
19 Haymarket Terr. **K16**
33 Hazelbank Terr. **K14**
33 Hazeldean Terr. **O13**
33 Hazelwood Gro. **P13**
19 Headrigg Row **O13**
19 Heart of Midlothian
  Stadium **K15**
18 Henderland Rd. **J16**
12 Henderson Gdns. **N19**
19 Henderson Pl. **M17**
19 Henderson Pl. La. **M17**
19 Henderson Row. **L17**
19 Henderson St. **N19**
19 Henderson Terr. **K15**
20 Henry Pl. **N15**
20 Henry St. **N15**
50 Hepburn Dr., *Dalk.* **V9**
24 Hercus Ln., *Muss.* **U15**
47 Herd Terr. **O8**
6 Heriot Bridge **M16**
  Heriot Cross*=Heriot
  Bridge
12 Heriot Hill Terr. **M18**
20 Heriot Pl. **M16**
6 Heriot Row **L17**
38 Heriot-Watt University &2
  D12, M16
30 Hermand Cr. **K14**
30 Hermand St. **J14**
30 Hermand Terr. **J14**
12 Hermiston Ho. **D13**
27 Hermiston Ho. Rd. **D13**
28 Hermiston Ct. **F13**
31 Hermitage Dr. **L13**
31 Hermitage Gdns. **L13**
31 Hermitage of Braid **L13**
13 Hermitage Pk. **O18**
13 Hermitage Pk. Gr. **O18**
13 Hermitage Park Sch. **O18**
13 Hermitage Park S. **O18**
12 Hermitage Pl. **O18**
31 Hermitage Terr. **L13**
12 Hibernian Stadium **O17**
41 High Buckstone **M11**
41 High Buckstone **M11**
6 High Riggs **L16**
20 High School Yards **N16**
7 High St. **M16**
49 High St., Bonnyrigg **R8**
49 High St., Lasswade **R9**
48 High St., Loanhead **P8**
50 High St., *Dalk.* **U10**
25 High St., *Muss.* **V15**

44 Highlea Circle **B8**
44 Highlea Gro. **B8**
22 Highway, The **Q16**
7 Hill Pl. **N16**
7 Hill Sq. **N16**
6 Hill St. **L17**
6 Hill St. La. N. **L17**
6 Hill St. La. S. **M17**
22 Hillcoat Ln. **R17**
22 Hillcoat Pl. **R17**
46 Hillend Country Pk. **L9**
  Hillend Pl.*=London Rd.
46 Hillend Ski Slope **L9**
49 Hillhead **R8**
9 Hillhouse Rd. **G18**
17 Hillpark Av. **G18**
17 Hillpark Brae **G17**
17 Hillpark Ct. **G18**
17 Hillpark Cr. **G17**
17 Hillpark Dr. **G18**
17 Hillpark Gdns. **G17**
17 Hillpark Gr. **G17**
17 Hillpark Ln. **H17**
17 Hillpark Rd. **G17**
17 Hillpark Terr. **G17**
17 Hillpark Way **H17**
17 Hillpark Wood **H17**
20 Hillside Cr. **N17**
20 Hillside St. **N17**
35 Hilltown Terr. **S13**
18 Hillview **H17**
16 Hillview Cr. **F16**
16 Hillview Dr. **F16**
16 Hillview Rd. **F16**
16 Hillview Terr. **F16**
19 Hilton National Edinburgh
  Hotel **K16**
30 Hollybank Terr. **K14**
11 Holy Cross Sch. **M19**
22 Holy Rood Sch. **P15**
20 Holyrood Ct. **N16**
21 Holyrood Pk. **O16**
20 Holyrood Park Rd. **N15**
7 Holyrood Rd. **N16**
7 Holyroodhouse, Palace of
  N16
19 Home St. **L15**
23 Hope La. **R16**
20 Hope Park Cr. **N15**
  Hope Park Sq.*=Meadow
  La.
20 Hope Park Terr. **N15**
25 Hope Pl., *Muss.* **W16**
6 Hope St. **L16**
19 Hope St. La. **L16**
31 Hope Terr. **M14**
12 Hopefield Terr. **N19**
20 Hopetoun Cr. **N17**
20 Hopetoun Cr. La. **N17**
12 Hopetoun St. **N18**
19 Horne Terr. **L15**
45 Horsburgh Bk. **C10**
45 Horsburgh Gdns. **C10**
45 Horsburgh Gr. **C10**
20 Horse Wynd **N16**
16 Hoseason Gdns. **F17**
35 Hosie Rigg **R15**
44 House of Cockburn **A8**
9 House o' Hill Av. **H18**
9 House o' Hill Brae **H18**
9 House o' Hill Cr. **H18**
9 House o' Hill Gdns. **H18**
9 House o' Hill Gro. **H18**
9 House o' Hill Gro. **H18**
9 House o' Hill Pl. **H18**
9 House o' Hill Rd. **H18**
9 House o' Hill Row **H18**
18 House o' Hill Terr. **H17**
6 Howard Hotel **M17**
11 Howard Pl. **M18**
11 Howard St **M18**
42 Howden Hall Ct. **N11**
42 Howden Hall Cr. **N11**
42 Howden Hall Dr. **N11**
42 Howden Hall Gdns. **O11**
42 Howden Hall Ln. **N11**
42 Howden Hall Pk. **N11**
42 Howden Hall Rd. **O11**

42 Howden Hall Way **O11**
42 Howden Pk. **N11**
7 Howden St. **N15**
40 Howe Pk. **K11**
6 Howe St. **M17**
19 Hugh Miller Pl. **L17**
50 Hunt Cl., *Dalk.* **U10**
48 Hunter Av. **P8**
7 Hunter Sq. **M16**
49 Hunter Terr. **R8**
48 Hunter Terr. **P8**
40 Hunter's Tryst **K11**
40 Hunter's Tryst Sch. **K12**
7 Huntly Ho. **N16**
11 Huntly St. **M18**
30 Hutchison Av. **J14**
30 Hutchison Cotts. **J14**
30 Hutchison Crossway **J14**
30 Hutchison Gdns. **J14**
30 Hutchison Gro. **J14**
30 Hutchison Ho. **J14**
30 Hutchison Ln. **J14**
30 Hutchison Medway **J14**
30 Hutchison Pk. **J14**
30 Hutchison Pl. **J14**
30 Hutchison Rd. **J14**
30 Hutchison Terr. **J14**
30 Hutchison Vw. **J14**
43 Hyvot Av. **P11**
43 Hyvot Ct. **P11**
43 Hyvot Gdns. **P11**
43 Hyvot Gr. **P11**
43 Hyvot Gro. **P11**
43 Hyvot Ln. **P11**
43 Hyvot Pk. **P11**
43 Hyvot Terr. **P11**
43 Hyvot Vw. **P11**
43 Hyvot's Bank Av. **Q11**
43 Hyvot's Bank Valley Pk. **P11**

18 Ice Rink, Murrayfield **J15**
33 Inch Nurseries **O13**
33 Inch Park, The **O13**
10 Inchcolm Ct. **J19**
10 Inchgarvie Ct. **J19**
12 Inchkeith Ct. **N18**
9 Inchmickery Ct. **H19**
10 Inchview Sch. **J18**
22 Inchview Terr. **Q17**
India Bdgs.*=Victoria St.
6 India Pl. **L17**
6 India St. **L17**
13 Industrial Rd. **O18**
Industry Home*=Industry La.
12 Industry La. **N19**
7 Infirmary St. **N16**
42 Inglewood Pl. **O12**
Inglis Ct.*=West Port
30 Inglis Green Rd. **H13**
14 Ingliston **A16**
33 Innocent Railway (walkway), The **O15**
8 Inveralmond Dr. **E19**
8 Inveralmond Gdns. **E19**
8 Inveralmond Gr. **E19**
47 Inveravon Rd. **O9**
24 Inveravon Terr., *Muss.* **V15**
25 Inveresk Brae, *Muss.* **V15**
25 Inveresk Cemetery, *Muss.* **V15**
25 Inveresk Ho., *Muss.* **V15**
25 Inveresk Ind. Estate, *Muss.* **V15**
24 Inveresk Mills Ind. Estate, *Muss.* **U15**
25 Inveresk Rd., *Muss.* **V15**
25 Inveresk Village Rd., *Muss.* **V15**
11 Inverleith Av. **L18**
11 Inverleith Av. S. **L18**
11 Inverleith Gdns. **L18**
11 Inverleith Gro. **K18**
11 Inverleith Ho. **L18**
11 Inverleith Pk. **L18**

11 Inverleith Pl. **L18**
11 Inverleith Place La. **L18**
11 Inverleith Row **L18**
11 Inverleith Terr. **L18**
11 Inverleith Terr. La. **L18**
50 Ironmill's Rd., *Dalk.* **T10**
12 Iona St. **N18**
33 Ivanhoe Cr. **O13**
30 Ivy Terr. **K15**

34 Jack Kane Centre **R14**
6 Jamaica St. **L17**
6 Jamaica St. N. La. **L17**
6 Jamaica St. S. La. **L17**
James' Ct.*=Lawnmarket
James Craig Walk*=Leith St.
32 James Gillespie's Sch. **M15**
19 James Gillespie's Sch. Annexe **L15**
50 James Lean Av., *Dalk.* **U10**
49 James Leary Way **S8**
23 James St. **S16**
23 James St. La. **S16**
25 James St., *Muss.* **V15**
12 Jameson Pl. **N18**
12 Jane St. **N18**
Jane Terr.*=Comely Green Cr.
42 Janefield **O10**
50 Jarnac Ct., *Dalk.* **U10**
7 Jawbone Walk **M15**
33 Jean Armour Av. **O13**
50 Jean Armour Dr., *Dalk.* **V9**
18 Jeffrey Av. **H17**
7 Jeffrey St. **N16**
23 Jessfield Terr. **M19**
23 Jewel and Esk Valley College, The **S15**
50 Jewel and Esk Valley Coll., The, *Dalk.* **T9**
34 Jewel Pk. **R15**
34 Jewel, The **R15**
21 Jock's Lodge **P17**
7 John Knox's Ho. **N16**
23 John St. **S16**
23 John St. La. **S16**
23 John St. La. W. **S16**
12 John's La. **O19**
12 John's Pl. **O19**
44 Johnsburn Gr. **B9**
44 Johnsburn Haugh **B9**
44 Johnsburn Pk. **B9**
44 Johnsburn Rd. **B9**
6 Johnston Terr. **M16**
23 Joppa Gdns. **S16**
23 Joppa Gro. **S16**
23 Joppa Pk. **S16**
23 Joppa Quarry Pk. **S16**
23 Joppa Rd. **S16**
23 Joppa Terr. **S16**
31 Jordan La. **L14**
14 Jubilee Rd. **A16**
12 Junction Pl. **N19**
38 Juniper Av. **F11**
38 Juniper Gdns. **F11**
38 Juniper Green Sch. **F11**
38 Juniper Green Sch. Annexe **F11**
38 Juniper Gro. **F11**
38 Juniper La. **F11**
Juniperlee*=Lanark Rd.
38 Juniperlee **F11**
38 Juniper Park Rd. **F11**
38 Juniper Terr. **F11**

17 Kaimes Rd. **G16**
43 Kaimes Sch. **P11**
51 Kaimes Vw. **R12**
39 Katesmill Rd. **H12**
12 Keddie Gdns. **N19**
42 Kedslie Pl. **N12**
42 Kedslie Rd. **N12**

6 Keir St. **M16**
17 Keith Cr. **H17**
18 Keith Row **J17**
17 Keith Terr. **H17**
22 Kekewich Av. **Q17**
27 Kellarstane **C14**
19 Kemp Pl. **L17**
42 Kenilworth Dr. **O12**
21 Kenmure Av. **P16**
47 Kennington Av. **O8**
47 Kennington Terr. **O8**
50 Kerr Av. **T9**
6 Kerr St. **L17**
25 Kerr's Wynd, *Muss.* **V15**
48 Kevock Rd. **Q8**
18 Kew Terr. **K16**
Kilchurn Ct.*=Craigievar Wynd
32 Kilgraston Ct. **M14**
32 Kilgraston Rd. **M14**
33 Kilmaurs Rd. **O14**
33 Kilmaurs Terr. **O14**
33 Kilncroftside **H13**
25 Kilwinning Pl., *Muss.* **V15**
25 Kilwinning St., *Muss.* **V15**
25 Kilwinning Terr., *Muss.* **V15**
18 Kinellan Rd. **J16**
20 King George V Pk. **M17**
47 King George's Field **O8**
49 King George's Park **R8**
20 King James Hotel **M17**
12 King St. **N19**
25 King St., *Muss.* **V15**
12 Kinghorn Pl. **M19**
6 King's Bridge **M16**
32 King's Bdgs., The **N13**
33 King's Haugh **P14**
23 King's Manor Hotel **S15**
50 King's Park Sch., *Dalk.* **U9**
50 King's Pk., *Dalk.* **U9**
22 King's Pl. **R17**
22 King's Rd. **R17**
6 King's Stables Rd. **L16**
6 King's Stables La. **M16**
22 King's Terr. **Q17**
6 King's Theatre **L15**
18 Kingsburgh Rd. **J16**
33 Kingsinch Sch. **O13**
29 Kingsknowe Av. **H13**
29 Kingsknowe Cr. **H13**
29 Kingsknowe Ct. **G13**
29 Kingsknowe Dr. **H13**
39 Kingsknowe Gdns. **H12**
39 Kingsknowe Golf Course **G12**
39 Kingsknowe Gro. **H12**
39 Kingsknowe Pk. **H12**
29 Kingsknowe Pl. **G13**
29 Kingsknowe Rd. N. **H13**
29 Kingsknowe Rd. S. **H13**
29 Kingsknowe Sta. **H13**
29 Kingsknowe Terr. **H13**
33 Kingston Av. **P13**
35 Kinnaird Pk. **S14**
11 Kinnear Rd. **K18**
50 Kippielaw Av., *Dalk.* **V9**
50 Kippielaw Gdns., *Dalk.* **V9**
50 Kippielaw Medway, *Dalk.* **V9**
50 Kippielaw Pk., *Dalk.* **V9**
50 Kippielaw Rd., *Dalk.* **V9**
50 Kippielaw Wk., *Dalk.* **V9**
33 Kirkbrae **O13**
8 Kirk Cramond **E19**
11 Kirk Ln. **G15**
42 Kirk Pk. **O12**
12 Kirk St. **N18**
Kirkgate, Leith*=Leith Walk
42 Kirkgate, Liberton **O12**
12 Kirkgate Ho. **O19**
33 Kirkhill Dr. **O14**
33 Kirkhill Gdns. **O15**
33 Kirkhill Rd. **O15**

33 Kirkhill Terr. **O15**
Kirklands*=Ladywell Av.
Kirkwood Pl.*=London Rd.
Kisimul Ct.*=Craigievar Wynd
32 Kittle Yards **N14**
35 Klondyke St. **T14**
35 Klondyke Way **T14**
50 Komarom Pl., *Dalk.* **V10**
Kyle Pl.*=Montrose Terr.

28 Labourfield **F13**
45 Lade, The **C8**
12 Ladehead **M18**
Ladiemeadow*=Roull Rd.
29 Lade Meadow **G15**
45 Lady Ct. **C9**
Ladyfield Pl.*=Morrison St.
6 Ladyfield Pl. **L16**
6 Lady Lawson St. **M16**
21 Lady Menzies Pl. **O17**
22 Lady Nairne Cr., **P16**
22 Lady Nairne Gro. **P16**
22 Lady Nairne Ln. **P16**
22 Lady Nairne Pl. **P16**
33 Lady Rd. **O14**
Lady Stair's Clo.*=North Bank St.
6 Lady Wynd **M16**
32 Ladysmith Rd. **N13**
25 Ladywell, *Muss.* **V15**
28 Ladywell Av. **F15**
16 Ladywell Gdns. **F15**
16 Ladywell Ho. **F15**
16 Ladywell Rd. **F15**
Ladywell Way*=North High St., *Muss.*
30 Laichfield **H14**
30 Laichpark Pl. **J14**
30 Laichpark Rd. **H14**
23 Laing Terr. **S16**
Lamb's Cl.*=East Crosscauseway
33 Lamermoor Terr. **P13**
29 Lampacre Rd. **G15**
39 Lanark Rd. **F13**
44 Lanark Rd. W. **A9**
47 Lang Ln. **O9**
47 Langloan Rd. **O9**
32 Langton Rd. **N14**
19 Lansdowne Cr. **K16**
12 Lapicide Pl. **N19**
44 Larch Gr. **B9**
44 Larchfield **C9**
Larchfield Neuk **C9**
12 Largo Pl. **N19**
49 Larkfield **S9**
49 Larkfield Dr. **S9**
49 Larkfield Rd. **T9**
43 Lasswade Bk. **P11**
43 Lasswade Gro. **P11**
50 Lasswade Rd. **T9**
42 Lasswade Rd. **O12**
48 Lasswade Rd., Lasswade **Q9**
48 Lasswade Rd., Loanhead **P8**
49 Lasswade Sch. **S8**
48 Lasswade Sch. **R8**
32 Lauder Ln. **N14**
32 Lauder Rd. **M15**
50 Lauder Rd., *Dalk.* **U9**
32 Lauderdale St. **M15**
50 Laurel Bk., *Dalk.* **V9**
31 Laurel Terr. **K15**
12 Laurie St. **O18**
9 Lauriston Castle **G19**
32 Lauriston Dental Centre **N14**
9 Lauriston Farm Rd. **G18**
20 Lauriston Gdns. **M15**
20 Lauriston Pk. **M15**
6 Lauriston Pl. **M16**
6 Lauriston St. **M16**
6 Lauriston Terr. **M16**
11 Laverockbank Av. **M19**

11 Laverockbank Cr. **M19**
11 Laverockbank Gdns. **M19**
11 Laverockbank Gro. **M19**
11 Laverockbank Rd. **M19**
11 Laverockbank Terr. **M19**
39 Laverockdale Cr. **H11**
39 Laverockdale Ln. **H11**
39 Laverockdale Pk. **H11**
Law Pl.*=Pipe St.
7 Lawnmarket **M16**
47 Lawrie Terr. **O8**
42 Leadervale Rd. **N12**
42 Leadervale Terr. **N12**
Leamington
  Pl.*=Leamington Terr.
12 Leamington Rd. **L15**
31 Leamington Terr. **L15**
19 Learmonth Av. **K17**
19 Learmonth Cr. **K17**
19 Learmonth Ct. **K17**
19 Learmonth Gdns. **K17**
19 Learmonth Gdns. La. **K17**
19 Learmonth Gdns. Mews **L17**
19 Learmonth Gro. **K17**
19 Learmonth Hotel **K17**
19 Learmonth Pk. **K17**
19 Learmonth Pl. **K17**
19 Learmonth Terr. **K17**
19 Learmonth Terr. La. **K17**
Learmonth
  Vw.*=Learmonth Terr.
7 Lecture Theatre **M16**
22 Lee Cr. **R16**
12 Leith **N19**
12 Leith Acad. **O18**
12 Leith Acad. Annexe **O18**
21 Leith Acad. Annexe **O17**
12 Leith Hosp. **N19**
12 Leith Links **O18**
12 Leith Sch. (Primary) **O18**
20 Leith St. **M17**
Leith St. Terr.*=Leith St.
20 Leith Walk **N17**
18 Leith Walk Sch. **N17**
18 Lennel Av. **J16**
15 Lennie Cotts. **C16**
15 Lennie Mains **C17**
15 Lennie Pk. **C16**
12 Lennox Row **L19**
19 Lennox St. **L17**
19 Lennox St. La. **L17**
14 Lennymuir **B17**
20 Leopold Pl. **N17**
21 Leslie Pl. **L17**
19 Leven St. **L15**
19 Leven Terr. **M15**
19 Lewis Terr. **L16**
25 Lewisvale Av. **W15**
25 Lewisvale Ct., *Muss.* **W15**
25 Lewisvale Pk., *Muss.* **V15**
49 Leyden Pk. **R8**
49 Leyden Pl. **R8**
33 Liberton Brae **O13**
42 Liberton Cem. **O12**
12 Liberton Dr. **N12**
42 Liberton Gdns. **O11**
33 Liberton Golf Course **P13**
43 Liberton Hosp. **O11**
42 Liberton Pk. **O12**
33 Liberton Rd. **O13**
43 Liberton Sch. **P12**
43 Liberton Sch. Annexe **P13**
33 Liberton Sch. (Primary) **O13**
42 Liberton Tower **N12**
19 Liddesdale Pl. **L17**
Lily Terr.*=Shandon Pl.
21 Lilyhill Terr. **P17**
14 Limes, The **L14**
13 Lindean Pl. **O18**
48 Linden Pl. **P8**
Lindsay Pl.*=Chambers St.
12 Lindsay Pl. **N19**
12 Lindsay Rd. **N19**
12 Lindsay St. **N19**

25 Linkfield Ct. **W15**
25 Linkfield Rd., *Muss.* **V15**
24 Links Av., *Muss.* **U16**
13 Links Gdns. **O19**
13 Links Gdns. La. **O19**
12 Links La. **O19**
12 Links Pl. **O19**
25 Links St., *Muss.* **V15**
25 Links Vw., *Muss.* **U16**
12 Linksview Ho. **O19**
21 Lismore Av. **P17**
21 Lismore Cr. **P17**
22 Lismore Sch. **Q15**
50 Little Acre, *Dalk.* **V8**
43 Little France Ho. **P12**
34 Little France Mills **P13**
Little France
  Mills*=Dalkeith Rd.
7 Lothian Bk., *Dalk.* **T9**
6 Little Lyceum **L16**
42 Little Rd. **O12**
11 Livingstone Pl. **M15**
11 Lixmount Av. **M19**
11 Lixmount Gdns. **M19**
47 Loan, The **O8**
48 Loanhead Cr. **P8**
48 Loanhead Hosp. **P8**
47 Loanhead Memorial Pk. **O8**
47 Loanhead Rd. **O9**
48 Loanhead Sch. **P8**
21 Loaning Cres. **P17**
21 Loaning Rd. **P17**
17 Loch Rd. **H17**
13 Lochend Av. **O18**
21 Lochend Castle Barns **O28**
Lochend Cl.*=Canongate
21 Lochend Dr. **P17**
21 Lochend Dr. **O17**
21 Lochend Gdns. **O17**
21 Lochend Gro. **P17**
21 Lochend Ho. **P17**
21 Lochend Pk. (street) **O17**
21 Lochend Pk. **O17**
21 Lochend Qt. **P17**
12 Lochend Rd. **O18**
21 Lochend Rd. S. **O17**
24 Lochend Rd. N., *Muss.* **U15**
24 Lochend Rd. S., *Muss.* **U15**
21 Lochend Sq. **O17**
19 Lochrin Bdgs. **L15**
6 Lochrin La. **L15**
19 Lochrin Pl. **L15**
Lochrin
  Terr.*=Thornybauk
20 Lochview Ct. **N16**
43 Lockerby Cotts. **P11**
43 Lockerby Cr. **P11**
43 Lockerby Gro. **P11**
30 Lockharton Av. **J13**
21 Lockharton Cr. **K13**
30 Lockharton Gdns. **K14**
32 Logan St. **M17**
21 Loganlea Av. **P17**
21 Loganlea Dr. **P17**
21 Loganlea Gdns. **P17**
21 Loganlea Loan **P17**
21 Loganlea Pl. **P17**
21 Loganlea Rd. **P17**
21 Loganlea Terr. **P17**
11 Logie Green Gdns. **M18**
11 Logie Green Loan **M18**
11 Logie Green Rd. **M18**
11 Lomond Rd. **L19**
7 London Rd. **N17**
50 London Rd., *Dalk.* **U10**
20 London St. **M17**
20 London St. Sch. **M17**
42 Longformacus Rd. **O12**
28 Long Hermiston **D13**
32 Longmore Hosp. **N15**
29 Longstone Av. **H13**
Longstone
  Cotts.*=Longstone Rd.
29 Longstone Cr. **H14**
29 Longstone Gdns. **G14**

29 Longstone Gro. **H13**
29 Longstone Pk. **H13**
29 Longstone Rd. **G13**
29 Longstone Sch. **H13**
29 Longstone St. **H13**
29 Longstone Terr. **G14**
29 Longstone Vw. **G14**
20 Lonsdale Terr. **M15**
24 Loretto Ct., *Muss.* **U14**
25 Loretto Playing Fields, *Muss.* **V16**
25 Loretto Sch., *Muss.* **V15**
Lord Russell
  Pl.*=Causewayside
12 Lorne Pl. **N18**
12 Lorne Sch. **N18**
12 Lorne Sq. **N18**
12 Lorne St. **N18**
50 Lothian Bk., *Dalk.* **T9**
50 Lothian Dr., *Dalk.* **V8**
6 Lothian Ho. **L16**
6 Lothian Rd. **L16**
50 Lothian Rd., *Dalk.* **U10**
7 Lothian St. **M16**
49 Lothian St. **S8**
46 Lothianburn Golf Course **L10**
44 Lovedale Av. **B9**
44 Lovedale Cr. **B9**
44 Lovedale Gdns. **B9**
44 Lovedale Gro. **B9**
44 Lovedale Rd. **C9**
32 Lovers' Ln. **M15**
49 Lower Broomieknowe **R8**
19 Lower Gilmore Pl. **L15**
11 Lower Granton Rd. **K20**
23 Lower Joppa **S16**
21 Lower London Rd. **O17**
17 Lufra Bk. **L19**
50 Lugton Brae, *Dalk.* **T10**
32 Lussielaw Rd. **N13**
20 Lutton Pl. **N15**
19 Lyceum Theatre **L16**
32 Lygon Rd. **N13**
17 Lyne St. **O17**
19 Lynedoch Pl. **L16**
19 Lynedoch Pl. La. **L16**
50 Lymphoy **D10**

25 Macbeth Moir Rd., *Muss.* **X15**
12 McDonald Pl. **M18**
12 McDonald Rd. **M18**
12 McDonald St. **N18**
32 McDowall Rd. **N14**
7 McEwan Hall **M16**
11 McKelvie Parade **L20**
19 McLaren Rd. **O14**
19 McLaren Terr. **L16**
18 McLeod St. **K15**
6 Mackenzie Pl. **L17**
47 Mckinlay Terr. **O8**
47 McNeill Av. **O8**
47 McNeill Pl. **O8**
19 McNeill St. **L15**
47 McNeill Terr. **O8**
49 McQuade St. **S8**
12 Madeira Pl. **N19**
12 Madeira St. **N19**
19 Magdala Mews **K16**
23 Magdalene Av. **R15**
22 Magdalene Ct. **R15**
22 Magdalene Dr. **R15**
23 Magdalene Gdns. **R15**
23 Magdalene La. **R15**
22 Magdalene Medway **R15**
23 Magdalene Pl. **R15**
18 Maidencraig Ct. **J17**
18 Maidencraig Cr. **J17**
18 Maidencraig Gro. **J17**
20 Main Point **M16**
9 Main St. **S8**
45 Main St., Balerno **C9**
Mains of Craigmillar*=
  Craigmillar Castle Rd.
24 Maitland Av., *Muss.* **U15**

24 Maitland Park Rd., *Muss.* **U15**
24 Maitland St., *Muss.* **U15**
37 Malcolmstone **D11**
25 Mall Av., *Muss.* **V15**
45 Malleny Av. **C8**
45 Malleny Ho. **C9**
45 Malleny Millgate **C8**
45 Malleny Pk. **C9**
Malta Gr.*=St. Bernard's Row
19 Malta Terr. **L17**
21 Mandela Theatre **N17**
12 Manderston St. **N18**
42 Mannering Pl. **O12**
19 Manor Pl. **L16**
17 Manse Rd. **F15**
16 Manse St. **F15**
25 Mansfield Av., *Muss.* **V15**
25 Mansfield Ct., *Dalk.* **V15**
20 Mansfield Pl. **M17**
25 Mansfield Pl., *Muss.* **V15**
25 Mansfield Rd., *Muss.* **V15**
45 Mansfield Rd. **C8**
32 Mansionhouse Rd. **M15**
17 March Gro. **G17**
17 March Pines **G17**
17 March Rd. **G17**
45 Marchbank Dr. **C8**
45 Marchbank Gdns. **C8**
45 Marchbank Gr. **C8**
45 Marchbank Wy. **C9**
Marchfield
  Gdns.*=Hillhouse Rd.
9 Marchfield Gro. **H29**
9 Marchfield Pk. **G18**
9 Marchfield Pk. La. **G18**
9 Marchfield Terr. **H17**
33 Marchhall Cr. **O15**
33 Marchhall Pl. **O15**
33 Marchhall Rd. **O15**
32 Marchmont Cr. **M15**
32 Marchmont Rd. **M15**
32 Marchmont St. **M15**
31 Mardale Cr. **L14**
9 Marine Dr. **G19**
13 Marine Esplanade **P19**
22 Marine Gardens Ind. Site **Q17**
21 Marionville Av. **O17**
21 Marionville Cr. **P17**
21 Marionville Dr. **P17**
21 Marionville Gro. **P17**
21 Merionville Medwy. **P17**
21 Marionville Pk. **O17**
21 Marionville Rd. **O17**
Marischal
  Pl.*=Queensferry Rd.
12 Maritime La. **O19**
12 Maritime St. **O19**
7 Market St. **M16**
24 Market St., *Muss.* **U15**
9 Markfield Park La. **G18**
23 Marlborough St. **R16**
33 Marmion Cr. **O13**
Marshall Pl.*=Kirkwood Pl.
7 Marshall St. **M16**
7 Marshall's Ct. **N17**
18 Martello Ct. **H19**
Martin's Ct.*=Bernard St.
49 Martin Gro. **S8**
49 Martin Pl., *Dalk.* **T9**
50 Maryburn Rd., *Dalk.* **V8**
18 Mary Erskine Sch. for Girls, The **H16**
21 Maryfield, Abbeyhill **N17**
22 Maryfield, Portobello **R17**
21 Maryfield Pl. **O17**
49 Maryfield Pl. **S8**
Mary's Pl.*=Raeburn Pl.
43 Marytree Ho. **P12**
32 Masson Hall **N14**
51 Massford Av. **R12**
32 Maurice Pl. **M13**
48 Mavis Bk. **P8**
50 Maxton Cr., *Dalk.* **U10**
31 Maxwell St. **L14**

9 May Ct. **H19**
24 May Pk., *Muss.* **U15**
Maybank Villas*=St.
John's Rd.
47 Mayburn Av. **O8**
47 Mayburn Av. **O9**
47 Mayburn Bk. **O8**
47 Mayburn Cr. **O9**
47 Mayburn Ct. **O8**
47 Mayburn Dr. **O9**
47 Mayburn Gro. **O8**
47 Mayburn Hill **O8**
47 Mayburn Ln. **O9**
47 Mayburn Terr. **O9**
47 Mayburn Vale **O8**
47 Mayburn Walk **O8**
16 Maybury Dr. **E16**
16 Maybury Rd. **E17**
24 Mayfield Av., *Muss.* **U14**
48 Mayfield Cr. **P8**
24 Mayfield Cr. **U14**
32 Mayfield Gdns. **N14**
32 Mayfield Gdns. La. **N14**
Mayfield Gdns. La.*=East Mayfield
Mayfield Pk., *Muss.* *=Mayfield Av.
Mayfield Pl.*=St. John's Rd.
24 Mayfield Pl., *Muss.* **U14**
32 Mayfield Rd. **N14**
32 Mayfield Terr. **N14**
47 Mayshade Rd. **O9**
11 Mayville Gdns. E. **M19**
20 Meadow La. **M15**
Meadow Pl.*=Roseneath Terr.
32 Meadow Pl. La. **M15**
28 Meadow Pl. Rd. **F15**
21 Meadowbank Av. **O17**
21 Meadowbank Cr. **O17**
Meadowbank Pl.*=London Rd.
21 Meadowbank Sports Centre **O17**
21 Meadowbank Terr. **O17**
15 Meadowfield **D16**
22 Meadowfield Av. **P16**
9 Meadowfield Ct. **P16**
21 Meadowfield Dr. **P16**
21 Meadowfield Gdns. **P15**
21 Meadowfield Terr. **P15**
42 Meadowhead **N12**
21 Meadowfield Pk. **P16**
17 Meadowhouse Rd. **G15**
37 Meadow Rd. **D12**
50 Meadow Spott, *Dalk.* **T9**
20 Meadows, The **M15**
16 Mearnside **E16**
7 Medical Sch. **M16**
28 Medwin Ho. **F13**
30 Meggetland Athletic Grd. **J14**
30 Meggetland Gate **J14**
30 Meggetland Terr. **K14**
Melbourne Pl.*=George IV Bridge
20 Melgund Terr. **M17**
6 Melville Cr. **L16**
49 Melville Castle Hotel **S9**
20 Melville Dr. **M15**
49 Melville Dykes **S9**
49 Melville Gate Rd. **S10**
51 Melville Grange **R10**
48 Melville Mains **R9**
51 Melville Nurseries **S10**
Melville Pl.*=Queensferry St.
Melville Terr.*=Dalhousie Rd.
19 Melville St. **L16**
19 Melville St. La. **L16**
32 Melville Terr. **M15**
49 Melville Vw. **R8**
22 Mentone Av. **R17**
32 Mentone Gdns. **N14**
32 Mentone Terr. **N14**

Merchant St.*= Candlemaker Row
31 Merchiston Av. **L15**
31 Merchiston Bank Av. **L14**
31 Merchiston Bk. Gdns. **L14**
39 Merchiston Castle Sch. **H12**
31 Merchiston Cr. **L14**
31 Merchiston Gdns. **K14**
30 Merchiston Gro. **K14**
31 Merchiston Mews **L15**
31 Merchiston Pk. **L15**
31 Merchiston Pl. **L15**
31 Mertoun Pl. **K15**
7 Meuse La. **M16**
31 Mid Gillsland Rd. **K14**
27 Mid Hermiston **D13**
33 Mid Liberton **O13**
28 Mid New Cultins **E13**
31 Mid Steil **K13**
47 Mid Straiton Cotts. **O9**
20 Middle Meadow Walk **M15**
26 Middle Norton **A15**
11 Middle Pier **K20**
32 Middleby St. **N14**
12 Middlefield **N18**
31 Midmar Av. **M13**
31 Midmar Dr. **M13**
31 Midmar Gdns. **L13**
32 Mill La. **N19**
31 Millar Cr. **L14**
31 Millar Pl. **L14**
31 Millar Pl. La. **L14**
19 Miller Row **L16**
32 Millerfield Pl. **M15**
35 Millerhill Rd. **R13**
25 Millhill, *Muss.* **V15**
25 Millhill La., *Muss.* **V15**
12 Milnacre **M19**
22 Milton Cr. **R15**
23 Milton Dr. **S16**
22 Milton Gdns. N. **R15**
22 Milton Gdns. S. **R15**
23 Milton Gro. **T16**
22 Milton Link **S15**
22 Milton Rd. **R15**
23 Milton Rd. E. **S15**
22 Milton Rd. W. **Q15**
21 Milton St. **O17**
23 Milton Terr. **T16**
32 Minto St. **N15**
12 Mitchell St. **O19**
50 Mitchell St., *Dalk.* **T10**
30 Moat Dr. **J14**
30 Moat Ho. **J14**
30 Moat Pl. **J14**
30 Moat St. **J14**
30 Moat Terr. **J14**
22 Moira Pk. **Q17**
22 Moira Terr. **Q17**
32 Moncreiff Terr. **N15**
43 Moncreiffe Ho. **P12**
42 Monkbarns Gdns. **O12**
24 Monkton Hall, *Muss.* **U14**
25 Monktonhall Golf Course **V14**
24 Monktonhall Hall Pl., *Muss.* **V14**
24 Monktonhall Ho., *Muss.* **U14**
24 Monktonhall Pl., *Muss.* **U15**
24 Monktonhall Terr., *Muss.* **U14**
32 Monkwood Ct. **M14**
11 Monmouth Terr. **L18**
7 Montague St. **N15**
11 Montagu Terr. **L18**
20 Montgomery Pl. E. **N17**
20 Montgomery Pl. W. **N17**
20 Montgomery St. **N17**
20 Montgomery St. La. **N17**
31 Montpelier **L15**
31 Montpelier Pk. **L15**
31 Montpelier Terr. **L15**
20 Montrose Terr. **N17**
35 Moorfield Cotts. **S12**

7 Moray House Coll. of Education **N16**
6 Moray Pl. **L17**
43 Moredun Dykes Rd. **P11**
43 Moredun Ho. **P12**
43 Moredun Institute (Animal Diseases) **P12**
43 Moredun Park Ct. **P12**
43 Moredun Park Dr. **P12**
43 Moredun Park Gdns. **P12**
43 Moredun Park Gr. **Q12**
43 Moredun Park Gro. **Q12**
43 Moredun Park Ln. **P12**
43 Moredun Park Rd. **P12**
43 Moredun Park St. **P12**
43 Moredun Park Vw. **Q12**
43 Moredun Park Walk **Q12**
43 Moredun Park Way **P12**
43 Moredun Sch. **P12**
43 Moredunvale Bk. **P12**
43 Moredunvale Gr. **P12**
43 Moredunvale Gro. **P12**
43 Moredunvale Ln. **P12**
43 Moredunvale Pk. **P12**
43 Moredunvale Pl. **P12**
43 Moredunvale Rd. **P12**
43 Moredunvale Vw. **P12**
43 Moredunvale Way **P12**
33 Morgan Athletic Grd. **O14**
31 Morningside Cem. **L13**
31 Morningside Ct. **L13**
31 Morningside Dr. **K13**
31 Morningside Gdns. **K13**
31 Morningside Gro. **K13**
31 Morningside Pk. (street) **L14**
31 Morningside Pk. **L13**
31 Morningside Pl. **L14**
31 Morningside Rd. **L14**
31 Morningside Terr. **L14**
19 Morrison Link **L16**
6 Morrison St. **L16**
19 Morrison St. Link **L16**
41 Morton Mains **M10**
23 Morton St. **S16**
42 Mortonhall Crem. **N11**
42 Mortonhall Garden Centre **N11**
42 Mortonhall Gate **N11**
41 Mortonhall Golf Course **M12**
42 Mortonhall Park Av. **N11**
42 Mortonhall Park Bk. **O11**
42 Mortonhall Park Cr. **O11**
42 Mortonhall Park Dr. **O11**
42 Mortonhall Park Gdns. **N11**
42 Mortonhall Park Gr. **N11**
42 Mortonhall Park Gro. **N11**
42 Mortonhall Park Ln. **N11**
42 Mortonhall Park Pl. **O11**
Mortonhall Pk. Terr.*=Mortonhall Pk. Dr.
42 Mortonhall Park Vw. **N11**
42 Mortonhall Park Way **N11**
32 Mortonhall Rd. **M14**
16 Morven St. **F17**
Mossgiel Walk*=Cumnor Cr.
32 Moston Terr. **N14**
6 Mound Pl. **M16**
6 Mound, The **M16**
43 Mount Alvernia Convent **O12**
32 Mount Grange **M14**
23 Mount Lodge Pl. **R16**
1 Mount Royal Hotel **M16**
43 Mount Vernon Cem. **O12**
42 Mount Vernon Rd. **O12**
6 Mountbatten Bdg. **M16**
22 Mountcastle Bk. **Q16**
22 Mountcastle Cr. **Q16**
22 Mountcastle Dr. N. **Q16**
22 Mountcastle Dr. S. **Q16**
22 Mountcastle Gdns. **Q16**
22 Mountcastle Gr. **Q17**

22 Mountcastle Gro. **Q16**
22 Mountcastle Ln. **Q16**
Mountcastle Pk.*=Mountcastle Cr.
22 Mountcastle Pl. **Q17**
22 Mountcastle Terr. **Q16**
41 Mounthooly Ln. **M11**
25 Mountjoy Terr., *Muss.* **V16**
24 Mucklets Av., *Muss.* **U14**
24 Mucklets Cr., *Muss.* **U14**
24 Mucklets Ct., *Muss.* **U14**
24 Mucklets Dr. **U14**
24 Mucklets Pl., *Muss.* **U14**
38 Muir Wood Cr. **E11**
38 Muir Wood Dr. **E11**
38 Muir Wood Gro. **E11**
38 Muir Wood Pl. **E11**
38 Muir Wood Rd. **E11**
18 Muirdale Terr. **H17**
39 Muirend Av. **G12**
Muirfield Gdns.*=The Loan
10 Muirhouse Av. **H18**
9 Muirhouse Bk. **H18**
10 Muirhouse Cr. **H19**
9 Muirhouse Dr. **H19**
9 Muirhouse Gdns. **H19**
9 Muirhouse Gr. **H18**
9 Muirhouse Gro. **H19**
9 Muirhouse Ln. **H19**
9 Muirhouse Medway **H18**
9 Muirhouse Pk. (street) **H18**
9 Muirhouse Pk. **H18**
9 Muirhouse Parkway **H19**
10 Muirhouse Pl. E. **H18**
10 Muirhouse Pl. W. **H18**
10 Muirhouse Sch. **H18**
10 Muirhouse Terr. **H18**
9 Muirhouse Vw. **H19**
10 Muirhouse Way **H18**
50 Muirpark **T9**
40 Muirside **K11**
Mulberry Pl.*=Newhaven Rd.
39 Munro Dr. **H11**
Munro Pl.*=Canonmills
20 Murano Pl. **N17**
32 Murchison Ho. **N13**
19 Murdoch Terr. **L15**
19 Murieston Cr. **K15**
19 Murieston Cr. La. **K15**
19 Murieston La. **K15**
19 Murieston Pl. **K15**
19 Murieston Rd. **K15**
19 Murieston Terr. **K15**
16 Murray Cotts. **F15**
8 Murray Gr. **F15**
43 Murray Home **P12**
28 Murrayburn Appr. **F13**
28 Murrayburn Dr. **F13**
28 Murrayburn Gate **F13**
29 Murrayburn Gdns. **G13**
29 Murrayburn Gr. **G13**
29 Murrayburn Gro. **G13**
28 Murrayburn Pk. **F13**
29 Murrayburn Pl. **F13**
29 Murrayburn Rd. **F13**
29 Murrayburn Sch. **G13**
18 Murrayfield Av. **J16**
18 Murrayfield Dr. **J16**
18 Murrayfield Gdns. **J16**
18 Murrayfield Golf Course **H16**
17 Murrayfield Hosp. **H16**
18 Murrayfield Ho. **J16**
18 Murrayfield Pl. **J16**
18 Murrayfield Rd. **J16**
18 Murrayfield (S.R.U. Grd.) **J15**
18 Murrayfield Stadium **J15**
43 Murrays, The **P10**
43 Murrays Brae, The **P10**
Museum of Childhood*=High St.
6 Music Hall **M16**
24 Musselburgh Burgh Sch., *Muss.* **V15**

25 Musselburgh Links, *Muss.* **V16**
25 Musselburgh Links Golf Course **W16**
25 Musselburgh Links Race Course **W16**
25 Musselburgh Loretto Sch., *Muss.* **V15**
23 Musselburgh Rd. **S16**
50 Musselburgh Rd., *Dalk.* **U10**
25 Musselburgh R.C. School **V15**
25 Musselburgh Sch., *Muss.* **V15**
31 Myreside Ct. **K13**
31 Myreside Rd. **K14**
30 Myrtle Terr. **K15**

13- Nantwich Dr. **Q18**
28 Napier Polytechnic (Sighthill Campus) **F13**
30 Napier Polytechnic (Craiglockhart Campus) **J13**
31 Napier Polytechnic (Merchiston Campus) **L14**
31 Napier Polytechnic (Spylaw Road) **K14**
31 Napier Polytechnic (Bryson Road) **K15**
32 Napier Polytechnic (Marchmont) **M15**
31 Napier Rd. **K21**
6 National Gallery **M16**
7 National Library of Scotland **M16**
32 National Library of Scotland-Scottish Science Library **N15**
49 Nazareth Ho. **R9**
Neidpath Ct.*=Craigievar Wynd
43 Nellfield **O12**
Nelson Pl.*=Dublin Meuse
6 Nelson St. **M17**
34 Nether Craigour **P13**
7 Nether Craigwell **N16**
38 Nether Currie Cr. **E11**
38 Nether Currie Pl. **E11**
38 Nether Currie Rd. **E11**
38 Nether Currie Sch. **E11**
15 Nether Lennie **C18**
7 Netherbow Arts Centre **N16**
11 Netherby Rd. **L19**
7 New Arthur Pl. **N15**
22 New Belfield **Q16**
12 New Bells Ct. **O19**
10 New Broompark **K20**
7 New Broughton **M17**
20 New Coll. **M16**
7 New John's Pl. **N15**
12 New La. **M19**
30 New Market Rd. **J14**
30 New Markets **J14**
30 New Mart Rd. **H14**
12 New Orchardfield **N18**
7 New St. Andrews Ho. **M17**
20 New St. **N16**
43 New St. **P11**
24 New St., *Muss.* **U15**
40 New Swanston **K11**
50 Newbattle Abbey, *Dalk.* **U9**
50 Newbattle Abbey Cres., *Dalk.* **T9**
50 Newbattle Abbey Hostel, *Dalk.* **U9**
50 Newbattle Golf Course, *Dalk.* **U9**
50 Newbattle Rd. **T9**
31 Newbattle Terr. **K15**
25 Newbigging, *Muss.* **V15**
35 Newcraighall Dr. **S14**

35 Newcraighall Ind. Estate **R14**
35 Newcraighall Pk. **T14**
35 Newcraighall Rd. **R14**
35 Newcraighall Sch. **T14**
11 Newhaven Main St. **M20**
12 Newhaven Pl. **M20**
12 Newhaven Rd. **M19**
24 Newhailes, *Muss.* **T15**
24 Newhailes Av., *Muss.* **U15**
24 Newhailes Cr., *Muss.* **U15**
24 Newhailes Rd., *Muss.* **U15**
36 Newhouse **B10**
33 Newington Cem. **O14**
32 Newington Rd. **N15**
12 Newkirkgate **N18**
Newlands Pk.*=Mayfield Gdns.
45 Newmills Av. **C10**
45 Newmills Cr. **C10**
45 Newmills Gro. **C10**
50 Newmills Rd., *Dalk.* **U10**
Newmills Terr.*=James Lean Av.
45 Newmills Rd. **C10**
6 Newport St. **L16**
43 Newtoft St. **Q11**
51 Newton Church Rd. **S12**
30 Newton St. **K15**
50 Newton St., *Dalk.* **V8**
51 Newton Village **S12**
7 Nicolson Sq. **N16**
7 Nicolson St. **N16**
35 Niddrie Cotts. **S14**
34 Niddrie Farm Gro. **Q14**
34 Niddrie House Av. **R14**
34 Niddrie House Dr. **R14**
34 Niddrie House Gdns. **R14**
34 Niddrie House Gro. **R14**
34 Niddrie House Pk. **Q14**
34 Niddrie House Sq. **Q14**
34 Niddrie Mains Ct. **R14**
34 Niddrie Mains Dr. **Q14**
34 Niddrie Mains Rd. **P14**
34 Niddrie Mains Terr. **Q14**
34 Niddrie Marischal Cr. **Q14**
34 Niddrie Marischal Dr. **Q14**
34 Niddrie Marischal Gdns. **Q14**
34 Niddrie Marischal Gr. **Q14**
34 Niddrie Marischal Gro. **R14**
34 Niddrie Marischal Ln. **Q14**
34 Niddrie Marischal Pl. **Q14**
34 Niddrie Marischal Rd. **R14**
34 Niddrie Marischal St. **Q14**
34 Niddrie Mill Av. **R14**
34 Niddrie Mill Cr. **R15**
34 Niddrie Mill Dr. **R14**
34 Niddrie Mill Gro. **R14**
34 Niddrie Mill Pl. **R14**
34 Niddrie Mill Terr. **R14**
34 Niddrie Policies **R14**
34 Niddrie Sch. **R14**
7 Niddry St. **M16**
Niddry St. S.*=Cowgate
42 Nigel Ln. **O12**
31 Nile Gro. **L14**
47 Niven's Knowe Rd. **N8**
47 Nivensknowe Caravan Park **N8**
13 Nisbet Ct. **O18**
13 Noble Pl. **O18**
8 North Bank St. **M16**
16 North Bridge **M16**
16 North Bughtlin Bk. **E17**
16 North Bughtlin Brae **E17**
16 North Bughtlin Gate **E17**
16 North Bughtlin Neuk **E17**
16 North Bughtlin Pl. **E17**
16 North Bughtlin Rd. **E17**
16 North Bughtlinfield **E17**
16 North Bughtlinrig **E17**
16 North Bughtlinside **E17**
33 North Cairntow **P15**

6 North Castle St. **L17**
6 North Charlotte St. **L16**
7 North Clyde St. La. **M17**
6 North East Circus Pl. **L17**
12 North Fort St. **N19**
34 North Greens **R15**
16 North Gyle Av. **E15**
16 North Gyle Dr. **E16**
16 North Gyle Farm Ct. **E15**
16 North Gyle Farm La. **E15**
16 North Gyle Gro. **E16**
16 North Gyle Ln. **E16**
16 North Gyle Pk. **E16**
16 North Gyle Rd. **E16**
16 North Gyle Terr. **E15**
24 North High St., *Muss.* **U15**
24 North High St., *Muss.* **V15**
12 North Hillhousefield **N19**
12 North Junction St. **N19**
12 North Leigh Mill **N19**
12 North Leigh Sands **N19**
20 North Meadow Walk **M15**
16 North Meggetland **K14**
30 North Merchiston Cem. **K15**
19 North Park Terr. **L17**
33 North Peffer Pl. **P14**
North St. Andrew La.*=N. St. Andrew St.
7 North St. Andrew St. **M17**
20 North St. David St. **M17**
31 North Walk, The **L13**
21 North Way, The **P16**
6 North West Circus Pl. **L17**
10 North Werber Pk. **K18**
10 North Werber Pl. **K18**
10 North Werber Rd. **K18**
50 North Wynd, *Dalk.* **U10**
19 Northcote St. **K22**
10 Northern General Hosp. **K18**
21 Northfield Av. **P16**
22 Northfield Bdwy. **P17**
22 Northfield Circus **P16**
22 Northfield Cr. **P16**
22 Northfield Dr. **Q16**
22 Northfield Farm Av. **Q16**
22 Northfield Farm Rd. **Q16**
22 Northfield Gdns. **Q16**
22 Northfield Gro. **Q16**
22 Northfield Pk. **Q16**
22 Northfield Park Gro. **Q16**
22 Northfield Rd. **P16**
22 Northfield Sq. **Q16**
Northfield Terr.*=Willowbrae Rd.
9 Northlawn Terr. **G18**
Northumberland Pl.*=Northumberland St.
6 Northumberland Pl. La. **M17**
6 Northumberland St. **M17**
6 Northumberland St. La., N.E. **M17**
6 Northumberland St. La., N.W. **M17**
6 Northumberland St. La., S.E. **M17**
6 Northumberland St. La., S.W. **M17**
10 Northview Ct. **H19**
21 Norton Pk. **O17**
26 Norton Mains **A15**
26 Norton Rd. **B14**

17 Oak La. **G17**
7 Oakfield **N15**
29 Oaklands Sch. **G14**
13 Oakville Terr. **O18**
32 Observatory Gr. **N13**
32 Observatory Rd. **N13**
33 Ochiltree Gdns. **P13**
7 Odeon Cinema **N15**
31 Ogilvie Terr. **K14**

Old Assembly Cl.*=High St.
7 Old Broughton **M17**
42 Old Burdiehouse Rd. **O10**
21 Old Church La. **P15**
33 Old Dalkeith Rd. **O14**
50 Old Dalkeith Rd., *Dalk* **T10**
50 Old Edinburgh Rd., *Dalk.* **T10**
40 Old Farm Av. **J12**
40 Old Farm Pl. **H12**
7 Old Fishmarket Cl. **M16**
17 Old Kirk Rd. **G16**
33 Old Mill La. **O13**
45 Old Newmills Rd. **C10**
47 Old Pentland **N9**
Old Quadrangle*=South Bridge
7 Old Tolbooth Wynd **N23**
7 Old Waverley Hotel **M16**
24 Olive Bank Pk., *Muss.* **U15**
24 Olivebank Rd., *Muss.* **U15**
18 Orchard Bk. **K17**
19 Orchard Brae **K17**
19 Orchard Brae Av. **K17**
19 Orchard Brae Gdns. **K17**
18 Orchard Brae Gdns. W. **K17**
19 Orchard Brae Ho. **K17**
Orchard Brae West*=Orchard Brae
18 Orchard Cr. **J17**
18 Orchard Dr. **J17**
18 Orchard Gdns. **J17**
19 Orchard Gro. **K17**
19 Orchard Pl. **K17**
18 Orchard Rd. **K17**
18 Orchard Rd. S. **J17**
18 Orchard Terr. **K17**
18 Orchard Toll **K17**
49 Orchard Vw. **T9**
17 Orchardfield Av. **F15**
12 Orchardfield La. **N18**
42 Orchardhead Ln. **O12**
42 Orchardhead Rd. **O12**
23 Ormelie Terr. **S16**
18 Ormidale Terr. **J16**
17 Ormiston Terr. **F15**
33 Orrock Pk. **O13**
19 Orwell Pl. **K15**
19 Orwell Sch. **K15**
19 Orwell Terr. **K15**
19 Osborne Terr. **K16**
32 Oswald Ct. **M14**
32 Oswald Rd. **M14**
16 Oswald Terr. **F15**
30 Otterburn Pk. **J12**
6 Outlook Tower and Camera Obscura **M16**
27 Over Gogar **C13**
9 Oxcars Ct. **H19**
11 Oxcraig St. **K20**
20 Oxford St. **N15**
19 Oxford Terr. **L17**
40 Oxgangs Av. **K11**
40 Oxgangs Bk. **K11**
40 Oxgangs Brae **K11**
40 Oxgangs Bdwy. **K11**
40 Oxgangs Cr. **K12**
40 Oxgangs Dr. **K12**
40 Oxgangs Farm Av. **K11**
40 Oxgangs Farm Dr. **K11**
40 Oxgangs Farm Gdns. **K11**
40 Oxgangs Farm Gro. **K11**
40 Oxgangs Farm Ln. **K11**
40 Oxgangs Farm Terr. **K11**
40 Oxgangs Gdns. **K12**
40 Oxgangs Gr. **K12**
40 Oxgangs Gro. **K12**
41 Oxgangs Hill **K12**
40 Oxgangs Ho. **K12**
40 Oxgangs Library **K11**
41 Oxgangs Ln. **K12**
40 Oxgangs Medway **K11**
40 Oxgangs Pk. **K11**
40 Oxgangs Path **K11**

40 Oxgangs Path E. **K11**
40 Oxgangs Pl. **K12**
40 Oxgangs Rise **K12**
40 Oxgangs Rd. **K11**
40 Oxgangs Rd. N. **J12**
40 Oxgangs Row **K11**
40 Oxgangs Sch. **J12**
40 Oxgangs St. **K11**
40 Oxgangs Terr. **K11**
40 Oxgangs Vw. **K11**

Paddock, The*=Balcarres
    Rd., Muss
17 Paddockholm **G15**
21 Paisley Av. **P16**
21 Paisley Cr. **P16**
21 Paisley Dr. **P16**
21 Paisley Gdns. **P16**
21 Paisley Gro. **P16**
21 Paisley Terr. **P16**
38 Palmer Pl. **D10**
38 Palmer Rd. **D11**
19 Palmerston Pl. **L10**
Palmerston Pl.
    La.*=Palmerston Pl.
32 Palmerston Rd. **M15**
50 Pankhurst Ln. **V10**
6 Panmure Pl. **M15**
47 Paradykes Av. **O8**
47 Paradykes Sch. **O8**
22 Park Av. **R16**
47 Park Av. **O8**
25 Park Av., Muss. **W15**
49 Park Cr. **R8**
47 Park Cr. **O8**
42 Park Cr. **O12**
25 Park Ct., Muss. **W15**
42 Park Gdns. **O12**
42 Park Gr. **O12**
25 Park Grove Pl. **W15**
25 Park Grove Terr., Muss.
    W15
25 Park House Day Hospital
    W15
25 Park La., Muss. **W15**
11 Park Pl. **M19**
11 Park Rd. **M19**
49 Park Rd. **R8**
50 Park Rd., Dalk. **T9**
35 Park Terr. **T14**
35 Park Vw. **S14**
47 Park Vw. **O8**
25 Park Vw., Muss. **W15**
22 Parker Av. **Q17**
22 Parker Rd. **Q17**
22 Parker Terr. **Q17**
16 Parkgrove Av. **F17**
16 Parkgrove Bk. **F17**
16 Parkgrove Cr. **F17**
16 Parkgrove Dr. **F17**
16 Parkgrove Gdns. **F17**
16 Parkgrove Gr. **F17**
16 Parkgrove Ln. **F17**
16 Parkgrove Neuk **F17**
Parkgrove
    Path*=Parkgrove Terr.
16 Parkgrove Pl. **F17**
16 Parkgrove Rd. **F17**
16 Parkgrove Row **F17**
16 Parkgrove St **F17**
16 Parkgrove Terr. **F17**
16 Parkgrove Vw. **F17**
29 Parkhead Av. **G13**
29 Parkhead Cr. **G13**
29 Parkhead Dr. **G13**
29 Parkhead Gdns. **G13**
29 Parkhead Gro. **G13**
29 Parkhead Ln. **G13**
29 Parkhead Pl. **G13**
29 Parkhead St. **G13**
29 Parkhead Terr. **G13**
29 Parkhead Vw. **G13**
50 Parkside Pl., Dalk. **U10**
7 Parkside St. **N15**
20 Parkside Terr. **N15**
25 Parsonage, Muss. **V15**
13 Parkvale Pl. **O18**

7 Parliament Ho. **M16**
Parliament
    Pl.*=Parliament St.
Parliament
    Sq.*=Newhaven Pl.
12 Parliament Sq. **M16**
7 Parliament St. **N19**
34 Parrotshot **R15**
21 Parsons Green Sch. **P16**
21 Parsons Green Terr. **P17**
40 Patie's Rd. **J12**
39 Patie's Rd. Recreation Grd.
    H12
Patriothall*=Hamilton Pl.
13 Pattison St. **O19**
12 Paulsfield **M8**
Peacock Ct.*=Newhaven
    Pl.
35 Peacocktail Cl. **R14**
16 Pearce Av. **F16**
16 Pearce Gro. **F23**
16 Pearce Rd. **F16**
29 Peatville Gdns. **H13**
29 Peatville Terr. **H13**
32 Peel Terr. **N14**
33 Peffer Bk. **P14**
33 Peffer Pl. **P14**
33 Peffer St. **P14**
33 Peffermill Ct. **P14**
33 Peffermill Ho. **P14**
33 Peffermill Rd. **O14**
34 Peffermill Sch. **P14**
8 Peggy's Mill Rd. **E18**
12 Pembroke Pl. **K16**
49 Pendreich Av. **S8**
49 Pendreich Dr. **S8**
49 Pendreich Gr. **S8**
49 Pendreich Terr. **S8**
49 Pendreich Vw. **S8**
10 Pennywell Cotts. **H19**
10 Pennywell Ct. **H19**
9 Pennywell Gdns. **H19**
9 Pennywell Gro. **H19**
9 Pennywell Medway **H19**
9 Pennywell Pl. **H19**
10 Pennywell Rd. **H19**
9 Pennywell Villas **H19**
37 Pentland Av. **D10**
28 Pentland Av. **H12**
30 Pentland Ho. **H12**
47 Pentland Caravan Park **N8**
41 Pentland Cr. **L12**
41 Pentland Dr. **K11**
41 Pentland Gdns. **L12**
41 Pentland Gro. **L12**
39 Pentland Hills **F10**
30 Pentland Ho. **J14**
47 Pentland Industrial Estate
    N8
47 Pentland Mains **N8**
38 Pentland Pl. **D10**
39 Pentland Rd. **H12**
48 Pentland Rd. **R8**
46 Pentland Rd. **M9**
41 Pentland Terr. **L12**
41 Pentland Vw., Comiston
    L11
50 Pentland Vw., Dalk. **V9**
38 Pentland Vw., Currie **D10**
38 Pentland View Ct. **D10**
12 Persevere Ct. **N19**
20 Perth St. **L17**
Pettigrew's Cl.*=St
    Andrews St., Dalk.
42 Peveril Terr. **O12**
7 Picardy Pl. **M17**
11 Pier Pl. **M20**
21 Piersfield Gro. **P17**
21 Piersfield Pl. **P17**
21 Piersfield Terr. **P17**
22 Piershill Cem. **Q17**
21 Piershill La. **P17**
21 Piershill Pl. **P17**
21 Piershill Sch. **P16**
21 Piershill Sq. E. **P17**
21 Piershill Sq. W. **P17**
21 Piershill Terr. **P17**
43 Pillars, The **P12**

12 Pilrig Cotts. **N18**
12 Pilrig Gdns. **N18**
12 Pilrig Ho. Cl. **N18**
12 Pilrig Pk. **N18**
21 Pilrig Park Sch. **N18**
Pilrig Pl.*=Pilrig St.
12 Pilrig St. **N18**
10 Pilton Av. **K19**
10 Pilton Cr. **K19**
10 Pilton Dr. **K19**
10 Pilton Dr. N. **K19**
10 Pilton Gdns. **K19**
10 Pilton Ln. **K19**
10 Pilton Pl. **K19**
17 Pinkhill **G15**
25 Pinkie Av., Muss. **W15**
25 Pinkie Dr., Muss. **W15**
25 Pinkie Hill Cr., Muss.
    W15
25 Pinkie Ho. **V15**
25 Pinkie Mains, Muss. **W15**
25 Pinkie Pl., Muss. **W15**
25 Pinkie Rd., Muss. **V15**
25 Pinkie Terr., Muss. **W15**
25 Pinkie St. Peter's Sch.,
    Muss. **W15**
22 Pipe La. **R17**
22 Pipe St. **R17**
13 Pirniefield Bk. **P18**
13 Pirniefield Gdns. **P18**
13 Pirniefield Gro. **P18**
13 Pirniefield Pl. **P18**
13 Pirniefield Terr. **P18**
10 Pirniehall Sch. **J19**
12 Pirrie St. **N18**
21 Pitlochry Pl. **O17**
31 Pitsligo Rd. **L14**
12 Pitt St. **N19**
Pittencrieff Ct.*=Craighall
    Terr.
23 Pittville St. **R16**
23 Pittville St. La. **R16**
50 Place Charente, Dalk. **V10**
Playfair Steps*=N. Bank
    St.
7 Playhouse **N17**
7 Pleasance **N16**
7 Pleasance Theatre **N16**
31 Plewlands Av. **K13**
31 Plewlands Gdns. **K13**
31 Plewlands Terr. **K13**
42 Pleydell Pl. **O12**
33 Pollock Halls **O15**
48 Polton Gdns. **R8**
48 Polton Ho. **Q8**
48 Polton Rd. **R8**
48 Polton Rd., Lasswade **R8**
49 Polton St. **R8**
31 Polwarth Cr. **L15**
31 Polwarth Gdns. **K15**
31 Polwarth Gro. **K15**
31 Polwarth Pk. **K15**
31 Polwarth Pl. **K14**
31 Polwarth Terr. **K13**
6 Ponton St. **L15**
13 Poplar La. **O19**
10 Porterfield Rd. **K18**
19 Portgower Pl. **L17**
Portland Pl.*=North
    Junction St.
Portland Terr.*=North
    Junction St.
12 Portland St. **N19**
23 Portobello Cem. **S15**
22 Portobello Golf Course
    R16
22 Portobello High St. **R17**
22 Portobello Rd. **P17**
22 Portobello Sch. **Q16**
22 Portobello Sch. Annexe
    R16
Portsburgh Sq.*=West
    Port
17 Post House Hotel **G15**
7 Post Office **M16**
7 Potterrow **M16**
Pottery, The*=Pipe La.

12 Powderhall Stadium **M18**
32 Preston St. Sch. **N15**
33 Prestonfield Av. **O14**
33 Prestonfield Bk. **O14**
33 Prestonfield Cr. **O14**
33 Prestonfield Gdns. **O14**
33 Prestonfield Golf Course
    O15
33 Prestonfield Pk. **O14**
33 Prestonfield Rd. **O14**
33 Prestonfield Sch. **O14**
33 Prestonfield Terr. **O14**
33 Priestfield Av. **O14**
33 Priestfield Cr. **O14**
33 Priestfield Gdns. **O14**
33 Priestfield Gro. **O15**
33 Priestfield Rd. **O15**
33 Priestfield Rd. N. **O15**
50 Primrose Cr., Dalk. **V9**
12 Primrose St. **O18**
30 Primrose Terr. **K15**
50 Primrose Terr., Dalk. **V9**
11 Primrose Bank Rd. **L19**
12 Prince Regent St. **N19**
6 Princes St. **L16**
6 Princess Alexandra Eye
    Pavilion **M15**
41 Princess Margaret Rose
    Hosp. **M11**
23 Promenade **R17**
24 Promenade **U16**
22 Promenade Terr. **R17**
13 Prospect Bank Cr. **O18**
13 Prospect Bank Gdns. **O18**
13 Prospect Bank Gro. **P18**
13 Prospect Bank Pl. **P18**
13 Prospect Bank Rd. **O18**
13 Prospect Bank Sch. **O18**
13 Prospect Bank Terr. **P18**
43 Protein Frac. Centre **P12**
49 Pryde Av. **R8**
48 Pryde Terr. **R8**

9 Quality St. **G18**
9 Quality St. La. **G18**
20 Quarry Cl. **N15**
35 Quarry Cotts. **R14**
Quarry Howe*=Deanpark
    Gro.
Quarryfoot
    Gr.*=Quarryfoot Gdns.
49 Quarryfoot Gdns. **R8**
49 Quarryfoot Pl. **R8**
12 Quarryhole Pk. **O18**
12 Quayside St. **N19**
Queen Charlotte
    La.*=Queen Charlotte
    St.
12 Queen Charlotte St. **O19**
17 Queen Margaret Coll. **F16**
6 Queen St. **L17**
6 Queen St. Gdns. **M17**
6 Queen St. Gdns. E. **M17**
6 Queen St. Gdns. W. **M17**
18 Queen's Av. **H17**
18 Queen's Av. S. **J17**
23 Queen's Bay Cr. **S16**
32 Queen's Cr. **N14**
21 Queen's Dr. **O16**
18 Queen's Gdns. **J17**
20 Queen's Hall, The **N15**
21 Queen's Park Av. **P17**
21 Queen's Pk. Ct. **P16**
18 Queen's Rd. **J17**
34 Queen's Walk **S14**
20 Queensberry Ho. **N16**
18 Queensferry Rd. **E18**
6 Queensferry St. **J16**
6 Queensferry St. La. **L16**
18 Queensferry Terr. **K17**
12 Quilts, The **N19**
12 Quilts Wynd **N19**

49 Rae's Gdns. **R8**
19 Raeburn Pl. **L17**
19 Raeburn St. **L17**

22 Ramsay Annexe
   (Stevenson Coll.) **Q17**
6 Ramsay Gdn. **M16**
6 Ramsay La. **M16**
22 Ramsay Pl. **R17**
6 Randolph Cliff **L16**
6 Randolph Cr. **L16**
6 Randolph Hall **L16**
6 Randolph La. **L16**
6 Randolph Pl. **L16**
7 Rankeillor St. **N15**
32 Rankin Av. **N13**
32 Rankin Dr. **N13**
32 Rankin Rd. **N14**
17 Rannoch Gro. **F17**
17 Rannoch Pl. **F17**
17 Rannoch Rd. **F17**
16 Rannoch Terr. **F17**
26 Ransfield **A13**
16 Ransome Gdns. **F17**
32 Ratcliffe Terr. **N14**
26 Ratho Park Golf Course
   B13
26 Ratho Park Rd. **A13**
44 Ravelrig Pk. **B9**
44 Ravelrig Rd. **B10**
44 Ravelrig Hill **B9**
18 Ravelston Ct. **J16**
18 Ravelston Dykes **J16**
18 Ravelston Dykes La. **H16**
18 Ravelston Dykes Rd. **H17**
18 Ravelston Gdn. **J16**
18 Ravelston Golf Course
   H17
18 Ravelston Heights **J17**
18 Ravelston House Gro. **J17**
18 Ravelston House Ln. **J17**
18 Ravelston House Pk. **J17**
18 Ravelston House Rd. **J17**
18 Ravelston Pk. (st) **K16**
18 Ravelston Pk. **H17**
   Ravelston Pl.*=Belford Rd.
18 Ravelston Rise **J16**
19 Ravelston Terr. **K17**
43 Ravenscroft Gdns. **Q11**
43 Ravenscroft Pl. **Q11**
43 Ravenscroft St. **Q11**
33 Ravenswood Av. **O13**
12 Redbraes Gdns. **M18**
12 Redbraes Pk. **M18**
12 Redbraes Pl. **M18**
40 Redford **J11**
40 Redford Av. **J11**
40 Redford Bk. **J11**
40 Redford Barracks **J12**
40 Redford Cr. **J11**
40 Redford Dr. **H11**
40 Redford Gdns. **J11**
40 Redford Gro. **J12**
40 Redford Ln. **J11**
40 Redford Neuk **J11**
40 Redford Pl. **J12**
40 Redford Rd. **J11**
40 Redford Terr. **J11**
40 Redford Walk **J11**
33 Redgauntlet Terr. **P13**
29 Redhall Av. **H13**
29 Redhall Bank Rd. **H13**
29 Redhall Cr. **H13**
29 Redhall Dr. **H13**
29 Redhall Gdns. **H13**
29 Redhall Gro. **H13**
30 Redhall House Dr. **H13**
29 Redhall Pk. **H13**
29 Redhall Pl. **H13**
29 Redhall Rd. **H13**
30 Redhall Vw. **H13**
28 Redheughs Av. **E14**
28 Redheughs Muir **E14**
28 Redheughs Rigg **E15**
28 Redheughs Rd. **D15**
   Reekies Ct.*=Nicholson
   St.
   Regent Bridge*=Waterloo
   Pl.
7 Regent Gdns. **N17**
21 Regent Pl. **O17**
7 Regent Rd. **N16**

7 Regent Road Pk. **N17**
23 Regent St. **R16**
23 Regent St. La. **R16**
7 Regent Terr. **N17**
7 Regent Terr. Mews **N17**
8 Regis Ct. **E18**
7 Register Ho. **M17**
7 Register Pl. **M17**
19 Reid Terr. **L17**
7 Reid's Cl. **N16**
   Reid's Ct.*=Canongate
32 Relugas Gdns. **N14**
32 Relugas Pl. **N14**
32 Relugas Rd. **N14**
37 Research Av. One **D12**
37 Research Av. Two **D12**
37 Research Park Rd. **D12**
21 Restalrig Av. **P17**
13 Restalrig Circus **P18**
13 Restalrig Cr. **P18**
21 Restalrig Dr. **P17**
21 Restalrig Gdns. **P17**
21 Restalrig Ho. **P28**
13 Restalrig Pk. **O18**
13 Restalrig Rd. **O18**
21 Restalrig Rd. S. **P17**
13 Restalrig Sq. **P18**
12 Restalrig Terr. **O18**
38 Riccarton Av. **D11**
38 Riccarton Cr. **E11**
38 Riccarton Dr. **D11**
38 Riccarton Gro. **E11**
38 Riccarton Mains **E12**
38 Riccarton Mains Rd. **E11**
38 Riccarton Sch. **D10**
7 Richmond La. **N16**
7 Richmond Pl. **N16**
19 Richmond Terr. **L16**
8 Riding Pk. **E18**
6 Riego St. **L16**
20 Rillbank Cr. **M15**
20 Rillbank Terr. **M15**
42 Ringwood Pl. **O12**
19 Rintoul Pl. **L17**
41 Riselaw Cr. **L12**
41 Riselaw Pl. **L12**
41 Riselaw Rd. **L12**
41 Riselaw Terr. **L12**
31 Ritchie Pl. **K15**
18 Riversdale Cr. **J15**
18 Riversdale Gro. **J16**
18 Riversdale Rd. **J16**
24 Riverside Gdns., *Muss.*
   U15
50 Roanshead Rd., *Dalk.* **V8**
30 Robb's Ln. **J14**
30 Robb's Loan Gro. **J14**
50 Robert Burn's Mews,
   Dalk. **V10**
33 Robert Burns Dr. **O13**
30 Robertson Av. **J15**
7 Robertson's Cl. **N16**
   Robertson's Cl., *Dalk.*
   *=St. Andrew St.
10 Rocheid Pk. **K18**
11 Rocheid Path **L18**
31 Rochester Terr. **L14**
49 Rockville Terr. **R8**
26 Roddinglaw **C14**
26 Roddinglaw Rd. **C14**
20 Rodney St. **M17**
8 Roman Fort (Rems.) **F19**
33 Romero Pl. **N15**
   Ronaldson's
   Wharf*=Sandport Pl.
11 Rose Pk. **L19**
6 Rose St. **L16**
6 Rose St. La., N. **L16**
6 Rose St. La., S. **L16**
12 Rosebank Cem. **N18**
6 Rosebank Cotts. **L16**
11 Rosebank Gdns. **L30**
11 Rosebank Gro. **L19**
11 Rosebank Rd. **L19**
19 Rosebery Cr. **K16**
19 Rosebery Cr. La. **K16**
19 Rosebery Ho. **K16**
18 Roseburn Av. **J16**

18 Roseburn Cliff **K16**
18 Roseburn Cr. **J16**
18 Roseburn Dr. **J16**
18 Roseburn Gdns. **J16**
18 Roseburn Pk. **J16**
18 Roseburn Pl. **J16**
18 Roseburn Sch. **J15**
18 Roseburn St. **J15**
18 Roseburn Terr. **J16**
22 Rosefield Av. **R16**
22 Rosefield Av. La. **R16**
22 Rosefield La. **R16**
22 Rosefield Pk. **R16**
22 Rosefield Pl. **R16**
22 Rosefield St. **R16**
6 Rosemount Bdgs. **L16**
32 Roseneath Pl. **M15**
32 Roseneath St. **M15**
32 Roseneath Terr. **M15**
13 Rosevale Pl. **O18**
13 Rosevale Terr. **O18**
11 Roseville Gdns. **M19**
32 Ross Gdns. **N14**
32 Ross Pl. **N14**
33 Ross Rd. **O13**
21 Rossie Pl. **O17**
12 Rosslyn Cr. **N18**
12 Rosslyn Terr. **N18**
19 Rothesay Mews **K16**
19 Rothesay Pl. **L16**
25 Rothesay Pl., *Muss.* **V15**
19 Rothesay Terr. **L16**
29 Roull Gro. **F15**
29 Roull Pl. **G15**
29 Roull Rd. **F15**
   Rowallan Ct.*=Craigievar
   Wynd
45 Rowan Tree Av. **D10**
45 Rowan Tree Gro. **D10**
45 Rowan Tree Pl. **D10**
7 Roxburgh Pl. **N16**
7 Roxburgh St. **N16**
   Roxburgh
   Terr.*=Drummond St.
6 Roxburghe Hotel **L16**
7 Royal Bank **M17**
32 Royal Blind Sch. **N14**
11 Royal Botanic Gdn. **L18**
7 Royal British Hotel **M16**
8 Royal Burgess Golf
   Course **E29**
6 Royal Circus **L17**
32 Royal Commonwealth
   Pool **N15**
20 Royal Cr. **M17**
32 Royal (Dick) Veterinary
   Coll. **N15**
31 Royal Edinburgh Hosp.
   L14
9 Royal High Sch., The **F18**
21 Royal High Sch., The
   (Primary) **P16**
14 Royal Highland Showgrd.
   A15
32 Royal Hospital for Sick
   Children **M15**
7 Royal Infirmary **M15**
7 Royal Mile Sch. **N16**
7 Royal Museum of
   Scotland (Chambers St.)
   M16
7 Royal Museum of
   Scotland (Queen St.)
   M17
32 Royal Observatory **M13**
21 Royal Park Pl. **O17**
21 Royal Park Terr. **O17**
16 Royal Scot Hotel **E15**
6 Royal Scottish Acad. **M16**
7 Royal Terr. **N17**
7 Royal Terr. Gdns. **N17**
7 Royal Terr. Hotel **N17**
7 Royal Terr. Mews **N17**
18 Royal Victoria Hosp. **K17**
10 Royston Mains Av. **J19**
10 Royston Mains Cr. **J19**
10 Royston Mains Gdns. **K19**
10 Royston Mains Gr. **K19**

10 Royston Ho. **J20**
10 Royston Mains Pl. **J19**
10 Royston Mains Rd. **K19**
10 Royston Mains St. **J19**
10 Royston Sch. **K19**
11 Royston Terr. **L18**
31 Rudolph Steiner Sch. **K14**
11 Russell Pl. **L19**
18 Russell Rd. **K16**
   Rustic Cotts.*=Colinton
   Rd.
33 Rutherford Dr. **O13**
6 Rutland Ct. **L16**
   Rutland Pl.*=West End
6 Rutland Sq. **L16**
6 Rutland St. **L16**
13 Ryehill Av. **O18**
13 Ryehill Gdns. **O18**
13 Ryehill Gro. **O18**
13 Ryehill Pl. **O18**
13 Ryehill Terr. **O18**

33 Saddletree Loan **P13**
9 Safeway Shopping Centre
   (Silverknowes) **G18**
21 Safeway Shopping Centre
   (Piershill) **P17**
32 St. Alban's Rd. **M14**
12 St. Andrew Pl. **O29**
7 St. Andrew Sq. **M17**
50 St. Andrew St., *Dalk.*
   U10
7 St. Andrew's Hotel **M17**
7 St. Andrew's Ho. **N17**
   St. Andrew Ct.*=St.
   Anthony St.
   St. Anthony La.*=St.
   Anthony St.
12 St. Anthony Pl. **N19**
12 St. Anthony St. **N19**
28 St. Augustine's Sch. **F14**
11 St. Augustine's Sch.
   Sports Grd. **L18**
43 St. Barnabas Ct. **Q12**
6 St. Bernard's Cr. **L17**
   St. Bernard's
   Pl.*=Saunders St.
19 St. Bernard's Row **L17**
6 St. Bernard's Well **L17**
17 St. Catherine's Gdns. **H15**
32 St. Catherine's Pl. **N15**
43 St. Catherine's Sch. **O11**
7 St. Cecilia's Hall **N16**
12 St. Clair Av. **O18**
12 St. Clair Pl. **O18**
12 St. Clair Rd. **O18**
12 St. Clair St. **O18**
31 St. Clair Terr. **K13**
6 St. Colme St. **L16**
11 St. Colm's Coll. **L18**
11 St. Columba's Hospice **L19**
32 St. Crispin's Sch. **N14**
30 St. Cuthbert's Sch. **J14**
   St. David's Pl.*=Morrison
   St.
10 St. David's Sch. **J18**
50 St. David's Sch., *Dalk.* **U9**
50 St. David's Sch. **V9**
   St. David's
   Terr.*=Morrison St.
31 St. Denis and Cranley Sch.
   K14
31 St. Fillan's Terr. **L13**
34 St. Francis' Sch. **Q14**
18 St. George's Sch. **K16**
7 St. Giles' Cathedral **M16**
29 St. Giles Centre **G14**
7 St. Giles' St. **M16**
7 St. James Centre **M17**
7 St. James' Pl. **M17**
   St. James' Pl.*=Cathedral
   La.
7 St. John St. **N16**
33 St. John Vianney Sch. **O13**
17 St. John's Av. **G15**
17 St. John's Cr. **G15**
17 St. John's Gdns. **G15**

St. John's Pl.*=Holyrood Rd.
16 St. John's Rd. **F15**
22 St. John's Sch. **R16**
17 St. John's Terr. **G15**
29 St. Joseph's Sch. **G14**
42 St. Katharine's Brae **O11**
42 St. Katharine's Cr. **O11**
42 St. Katharine's Ln. **O11**
7 St. Leonard's Bk. **N15**
7 St. Leonard's Crag **N15**
7 St. Leonard's Hill **N15**
7 St. Leonard's La. **N15**
20 St. Leonard's St. **N15**
16 St. Margaret's Pk. **F15**
32 St. Margaret's Rd. **L14**
47 St. Margaret's Sch. **P9**
33 St. Margaret's Sch. **O14**
33 St. Margaret's Sch. Senior Coll. **O14**
23 St. Mark's La. **R16**
12 St. Mark's Pk. **M18**
23 St. Mark's Pl. **R16**
40 St. Mark's Sch. **K12**
6 St. Mary's Cathedral (Episc.) **L16**
7 St. Mary's Cathedral (R.C.) **M17**
6 St. Mary's Music Sch. **L16**
23 St. Mary's Pl. **S16**
7 St. Mary's Sch. **M17**
13 St. Mary's Sch., Leith **O19**
7 St. Mary's St. **N16**
25 St. Michael's Av., *Muss.* **V15**
30 St. Nicholas' Sch. **J15**
16 St. Ninian's Dr. **F16**
17 St. Ninian's Rd. **F16**
21 St. Ninian's Sch. **P17**
31 St. Ninian's Terr. **K13**
7 St. Patrick Sq. **N15**
7 St. Patrick St. **N15**
St. Patrick Sch.*=Cowgate
7 St. Patrick's Sch. **N16**
St. Peter's Bdgs.*=Gilmore Pl.
19 St. Peter's Pl. **L15**
31 St. Peter's Sch. **L14**
20 St. Peter's Sch. Annexe **M15**
32 St. Raphael's **M14**
31 St. Ronan's Terr. **L13**
18 St. Serf's Sch. **K16**
St. Stephen Pl.*=St. Stephen St.
19 St. Stephen St. **L17**
31 St. Teresa's Pl. **K14**
6 St. Thomas of Aquin's Sch. **M15**
32 St. Thomas Rd. **M14**
6 St. Vincent St. **L17**
13 Salamander Pl. **O19**
13 Salamander St. **O19**
32 Salisbury Pl. **N15**
32 Salisbury Rd. **N15**
21 Salmond Pl. **O17**
50 Salters Rd., *Dalk.* **V10**
50 Salter's Gr., *Dalk.* **V10**
50 Salter's Terr., *Dalk.* **V10**
Saltire Society*=High St.
9 Salvesen Cr. **H19**
9 Salvesen Gdns. **H19**
9 Salvesen Gro. **H19**
9 Salvesen Terr. **H19**
22 Sandford Gdns. **R16**
12 Sandport **O19**
12 Sandport Pl. **N19**
12 Sandport St. **N19**
19 Sauchiebank **K15**
30 Saughton Av. **J15**
30 Saughton Cem. **H14**
17 Saughton Cr. **H15**
17 Saughton Gdns. **H15**
17 Saughton Gro. **H15**
17 Saughton Ln. **H15**
29 Saughton Mains Av. **G14**
29 Saughton Mains Bk. **H14**

Saughton Mains Cotts.*= Saughton Mains Gdns.
29 Saughton Mains Dr. **G14**
29 Saughton Mains Gdns. **G14**
29 Saughton Mains Gro. **H14**
29 Saughton Mains Ln. **G14**
29 Saughton Mains Pk. **G14**
29 Saughton Mains Pl. **G14**
29 Saughton Mains St. **G14**
29 Saughton Mains Terr. **G14**
17 Saughton Pk. (st.) **H15**
30 Saughton Pk. **H15**
29 Saughton Prison **H14**
29 Saughton Rd. **G14**
29 Saughton Rd. N. **G15**
18 Saughtonhall Av. **H15**
18 Saughtonhall Av. W. **H15**
18 Saughtonhall Circus **J15**
18 Saughtonhall Cr. **H15**
18 Saughtonhall Dr. **H15**
18 Saughtonhall Gdns. **J15**
18 Saughtonhall Gro. **J15**
18 Saughtonhall Pl. **H15**
18 Saughtonhall Terr. **J15**
19 Saunders St. **L17**
32 Savile Pl. **N14**
32 Savile Terr. **N14**
19 Saxe-Coburg Pl. **L17**
19 Saxe-Coburg St. **L17**
Saxe-Coburg Terr.*= Saxe-Coburg St.
8 School Brae **E19**
48 School Brae **R9**
49 School Gr. **R9**
32 Sciennes **N15**
Sciennes Hill Pl.*=Sciennes
Sciennes House Dr.*=Sciennes
32 Sciennes House Pl. **N15**
32 Sciennes Pl. **N15**
32 Sciennes Rd. **M15**
32 Sciennes Sch. **M15**
Sciennes St. E.*=Causewayside
49 Scollon Av. **S8**
21 Scone Gdns. **P17**
6 Scotch Whisky Heritage Centre **M16**
20 Scotland St. **M17**
20 Scotland St. La. E. **M17**
20 Scotland St. La. W. **M17**
7 Scott Monument **M16**
6 Scottish Experience, The **L16**
11 Scottish Gall. **L16**
11 Scottish Marine Biological Association **M19**
19 Scottish National Gall. of Modern Art **K16**
7 Scottish National Portrait Gall. **M17**
7 Scottish Poetry Library **N16**
7 Scottish Travel Centre **M17**
20 Scottish Widows **N15**
31 Scottish Youth Hostel Association Office **L15**
17 Scottish Zoological Pk. **G16**
13 Seacot **P18**
13 Seafield Av. **P18**
13 Seafield Cem. **P18**
13 Seafield Crem. **P18**
22 Seafield Ind. Estate **Q17**
13 Seafield Pl. **P18**
46 Seafield Moor Rd. **M9**
13 Seafield Recreation Grd. **Q18**
13 Seafield Rd. **P18**
22 Seafield Rd. E. **Q17**
13 Seafield St. **P18**
Seafield Terr.*=Seafield Av.
13 Seafield Way **Q18**
18 Seaforth Dr. **J17**

18 Seaforth Terr. **J17**
10 Sealcar St. **K20**
Seaport St.*=Bernard St.
23 Seaview Cr. **S16**
23 Seaview Terr. **S16**
37 Second Gait **D12**
6 Semple St. **L16**
32 Seton Pl. **N15**
50 Shadepark Cr., *Dalk.* **U10**
50 Shadepark Dr., *Dalk.* **U10**
50 Shadepark Gdns., *Dalk.* **U10**
30 Shaftesbury Pk. **K14**
30 Shandon Cr. **K14**
30 Shandon Pl. **K14**
30 Shandon Rd. **K14**
30 Shandon St. **K14**
30 Shandon Terr. **K14**
6 Shandwick Pl. **L16**
33 Shanter Way **O13**
33 Sharpdale Ln. **O14**
33 Shaw's Pl. **N18**
12 Shaw's Sq.*=Gayfield Sq.
12 Shaw's St. **N18**
12 Shaw's Terr. **N18**
6 Sheraton Hotel **L16**
12 Sheriff Brae **N19**
7 Sheriff Ct. **M16**
12 Sheriff Pk. **N19**
12 Shore **O19**
12 Shore Pl. **O19**
25 Shorthope St., *Muss.* **V15**
22 Shrub Mount **R17**
20 Shrub Pl. **N17**
Shrub Pl. La.*=Shrub Pl.
32 Sienna Gdns. **N15**
29 Sighthill Av. **G13**
28 Sighthill Bk. **F13**
28 Sighthill Ct. **F13**
28 Sighthill Cr. **F13**
28 Sighthill Dr. **F13**
29 Sighthill Gdns. **F13**
28 Sighthill Gr. **F13**
29 Sighthill Gro. **G13**
28 Sighthill Health Centre **F13**
28 Sighthill Ind. Estate **E14**
28 Sighthill Ln. **F13**
28 Sighthill Neuk **F13**
29 Sighthill Pk. (st.) **F13**
28 Sighthill Pk. **F14**
28 Sighthill Pl. **F13**
28 Sighthill Rise **F13**
28 Sighthill Rd. **F13**
28 Sighthill Sch. **F13**
28 Sighthill St. **F13**
28 Sighthill Terr. **F13**
28 Sighthill Vw. **F13**
28 Sighthill Wynd **F13**
9 Silverknowes Av. **G18**
9 Silverknowes Bk. **G18**
9 Silverknowes Brae **G18**
9 Silverknowes Ct. **G18**
9 Silverknowes Cr. **G18**
9 Silverknowes Dell **G18**
9 Silverknowes Dr. **G18**
9 Silverknowes Eastway **G18**
9 Silverknowes Gdns. **G19**
9 Silverknowes Golf Course **G19**
9 Silverknowes Gr. **H18**
9 Silverknowes Gro. **G18**
9 Silverknowes Hill **G18**
9 Silverknowes Ln. **G18**
9 Silverknowes Midway **H29**
9 Silverknowes Neuk **H18**
9 Silverknowes Pk. **G19**
9 Silverknowes Parkway **G19**
9 Silverknowes Pl. **G19**
9 Silverknowes Rd. **G19**
9 Silverknowes Rd. E. **G18**
9 Silverknowes Rd. S. **G18**
9 Silverknowes Sch. **H18**
9 Silverknowes Southway **H18**
9 Silverknowes Terr. **G18**

9 Silverknowes Vw. **H18**
7 Simon Sq. **N16**
6 Simpson Memorial Maternity Pavilion **M15**
22 Sir Harry Lauder Rd. **R16**
45 Slaeside **C9**
30 Slateford Rd. **J14**
30 Slateford Sta. **J14**
21 Sleigh Dr. **O17**
21 Sleigh Gdns. **P17**
12 Sloan St. **N18**
25 Smeaton Gro. **V14**
30 Smithfield St. **J15**
12 Smith's Pl. **N18**
51 Smithy Green Av. **R12**
Society*=Chambers St.
Solicitor's Bdgs.*=Cowgate
13 Somerset Pl. **O18**
40 Sour Howe **K11**
9 South Barnton Av. **G18**
17 South Beechwood **H15**
7 South Bridge **M16**
6 South Charlotte St. **L16**
20 South Clerk St. **N15**
7 South College St. **M16**
6 South East Circus Pl. **L17**
31 South Ettrick Rd. **K14**
12 South Fort St. **N19**
South Gayfield La.*=Gayfield Sq.
31 South Gillsland Rd. **K14**
32 South Gray St. **N14**
7 South Gray's Cl. **N16**
18 South Groathill Av. **J17**
28 South Gyle Access **F14**
28 South Gyle Bdwy. **E14**
28 South Gyle Cres. **E14**
28 South Gyle Gdns. **E15**
28 South Gyle Ln. **E15**
28 South Gyle Mains **E15**
28 South Gyle Pk. **E15**
28 South Gyle Rd. **F15**
28 South Gyle Sta. **E15**
28 South Gyle Wynd **F14**
32 South Lauder Rd. **N14**
11 South Laverockbank Av. **M19**
19 South Learmonth Av. **K17**
19 South Learmonth Gdns. **K17**
12 South Lorne Pl. **N18**
16 South Maybury **E15**
South Meadow Walk*=Meadow Pl.
22 South Mellis Pk. **Q16**
31 South Morningside Sch. **L13**
23 South Morton St. **S16**
32 South Oswald Rd. **M14**
32 South Oxford St. **N15**
11 South Pk. **M19**
7 South St. Andrew St. **M17**
7 South St. David St. **M16**
24 South St., *Muss.* **U15**
50 South St., *Dalk.* **U10**
12 South Sloan St. **N18**
11 South Trinity Rd. **L19**
22 Southfield Bk. **Q15**
22 Southfield Farm Gro. **Q16**
22 Southfield Gdns. E. **Q16**
22 Southfield Gdns. W. **Q16**
43 Southfield Hosp. **P12**
22 Southfield Ln. **Q15**
22 Southfield Pl. **R16**
Southfield Pl. N.*=Southfield Sq.
Southfield Pl. S.*=Southfield Sq.
22 Southfield Rd. E. **Q15**
22 Southfield Rd. W. **Q15**
22 Southfield Sq. **Q15**
22 Southfield Terr. **Q15**
Southfield Villas*=Stanley St.
42 Southhouse Av. **O11**
42 Southhouse Bdwy. **O10**
43 Southhouse Cr. **O10**

42 Southhouse Gdns. O10
42 Southhouse Gro. O10
43 Southhouse Medway O11
43 Southhouse Paths O11
42 Southhouse Rd. O11
43 Southhouse Sq. O10
43 Southhouse Terr. P11
43 Soutra Ct. O11
22 Spa Pl. R17
50 Spalding Cr., *Dalk.* U10
33 Spence St. N15
11 Spencer Pl. L19
12 Spey St. N18
12 Spey St. La. N18
12 Spey Terr. N18
12 Spiers Pl. N19
43 Spinney, The P11
6 Spittal St. L16
Spittalfield Cr.*=St. Leonard's St.
32 Spottiswoode Rd. M15
32 Spottiswoode St. M15
21 Spring Gdns. O17
Springfield Bdgs.*=Springfield St.
12 Springfield N18
12 Springfield St. N18
31 Springvalley Gdns. L14
31 Springvalley Terr. L14
31 Springwell Ho. Health Centre K15
19 Springwell Pl. K15
42 Springwood Pk. O12
39 Spylaw Av. G12
39 Spylaw Bank Rd. G12
39 Spylaw Ho. H11
39 Spylaw Pk. (street) G12
39 Spylaw Pk. H11
31 Spylaw Rd. K14
39 Spylaw St. H11
51 Square, The R12
31 Stable La. L14
6 Stafford St. L16
18 Stair Pk. J16
9 Stakis Commodore G20
6 Stakis Grosvenor Hotel L16
42 Stanedykehead N11
19 Stanhope Pl. K16
Stanhope Pl. W.*=Stanhope Pl.
19 Stanhope St. K16
21 Stanley Pl. O17
11 Stanley Rd. M19
22 Stanley St. R16
22 Stanwell St. N18
22 Stapeley Av. Q17
11 Starbank Pk. M19
11 Starbank Rd. M19
40 Stark's Cotts. K12
22 Station Brae R16
45 Station Ln. C10
17 Station Rd. G15
48 Station Rd. P8
50 Station Rd., *Dalk.* T9
24 Station Rd., *Muss.* U15
12 Stead's Pl. N18
31 Steils, The K12
31 Steel's Pl. L14
29 Stenhouse Av. H14
29 Stenhouse Av. W. H14
29 Stenhouse Cotts., H14
29 Stenhouse Cr. H14
29 Stenhouse Cross H14
29 Stenhouse Dr. G14
29 Stenhouse Gdns. H14
29 Stenhouse Gdns. N. H14
29 Stenhouse Gro. H14
29 Stenhouse Mill Cr. H14
29 Stenhouse Mill La. H14
29 Stenhouse Mill Wynd H14
29 Stenhouse Pl. E. H14
29 Stenhouse Pl. W. H14
29 Stenhouse Rd. H14
29 Stenhouse Sch. H14
29 Stenhouse St. E. H14
29 Stenhouse St. W. G14
29 Stenhouse Terr. H14

Stevenlaw's Cl.*=High St.
30 Stevenson Av. J15
28 Stevenson Coll. of Further Education F14
29 Stevenson Dr. H14
30 Stevenson Gro. J15
30 Stevenson Rd. J15
30 Stevenson Terr. J15
37 Stewart Av. D10
37 Stewart Cr. D10
37 Stewart Gdns. D10
37 Stewart Pl. D10
37 Stewart Rd. D10
12 Stewartfield M18
30 Stewart Terr. J15
19 Stewart's Melville Coll. K17
11 Stewart's Melville Coll. Sports Grd. K18
11 Stirling Rd. L19
6 Stockbridge Health Centre L17
19 Stockbridge Sch. L17
24 Stoneybank Av., *Muss.* U14
24 Stoneybank Cr., *Muss.* U14
24 Stoneybank Ct., *Muss.* U15
24 Stoneybank Dr., *Muss.* U15
24 Stoneybank Gdns., *Muss.* U15
24 Stoneybank Gdns. N., *Muss.* U15
24 Stoneybank Gdns. S., *Muss.* U14
24 Stoneybank Gr., *Muss.* U14
24 Stoneybank Pl., *Muss.* U14
24 Stoneybank Rd., *Muss.* U14
24 Stoneybank Terr., *Muss.* U14
24 Stoneyhill Av., *Muss.* U15
24 Stoneyhill Cr., *Muss.* U15
24 Stoneyhill Ct. U15
24 Stoneyhill Dr., *Muss.* U15
24 Stoneyhill Farm Rd., *Muss.* U15
24 Stoneyhill Gr., *Muss.* U15
24 Stoneyhill Ho. U15
24 Stoneyhill Pl., *Muss.* U15
24 Stoneyhill Rise, *Muss.* U15
24 Stoneyhill Rd., *Muss.* U15
24 Stoneyhill Terr., *Muss.* U15
24 Stoneyhill Wynd, *Muss.* U15
Storrie's Alley*=Giles St.
17 Strachan Gdns. H17
18 Strachan Rd. H17
23 Straiton Pl. R16
47 Straiton O9
47 Straiton Caravan Park O9
47 Straiton Rd. N8
8 Strathalmond Ct. D18
8 Strathalmond Gr. D29
8 Strathalmond Pk. D17
15 Strathalmond Rd. D17
31 Strathearn Pl. L14
32 Strathearn Rd. M14
32 Strathfillan Rd. M14
50 Strawberry Bk. T9
16 Stuart Cres. E16
16 Stuart Gr. E16
16 Stuart Pk. E16
16 Stuart Sq. E16
16 Stuart Wynd E16
7 Student Centre M16
18 Succoth Av. J16
18 Succoth Ct. J16
18 Succoth Gdns. J16
18 Succoth Pk. J16

18 Succoth Pl. J16
32 Suffolk Rd. N14
20 Summer Bk. M17
11 Summer Pl. M18
33 Summer Trees Ct. O13
13 Summerfield Gdns. O18
13 Summerfield Pl. O18
32 Summerhall N15
Summerhall Pl.*=Causewayside
32 Summerhall Sq. N15
12 Summerside Pl. M19
12 Summerside St. M19
16 Sunbury Mews K16
19 Sunbury Pl. K16
19 Sunbury St. K16
21 Sunnybank Pl. O17
21 Sunnybank Terr. O17
21 Sunnyside O17
Surgeon Sq.*=Infirmary St.
7 Surgeons' Hall N16
Surrey Pl.*=Borthwick Pl.
Surrey Sq.*=Sutherland St.
19 Sutherland St. K16
41 Swan Spring Av. L12
12 Swanfield M18
41 Swanston Av. L11
41 Swanston Cr. L11
41 Swanston Cott. K10
41 Swanston Cotts. L10
41 Swanston Dr. L10
41 Swanston Gdns. L11
41 Swanston Golf Course K10
41 Swanston Gr. L11
41 Swanston Gro. L10
40 Swanston Ho. K10
41 Swanston Ln. L11
41 Swanston Muir K11
41 Swanston Pk. L11
41 Swanston Pl. L11
41 Swanston Rd. L10
41 Swanston Row L11
41 Swanston Terr. L11
41 Swanston Vw. L11
41 Swanston Way L11
Sycamore Gdns.*= Saughton Rd. N.
17 Sycamore Terr G15
22 Sydney Pk. Q17
22 Sydney Pl. Q17
22 Sydney Terr. Q17
20 Sylvan Pl. M15
32 Synagogue N15

50 Tait St., *Dalk.* U10
7 Talbot Rice Art Gall. M16
33 Talisman Pl. Q17
11 Tanfield M18
11 Tanfield La. M18
32 Tantallon Pl. N15
7 Tarvit St. L16
12 Tay St. K15
12 Taylor Gdns. N19
21 Taylor Pl. O17
50 Taylor Pl., *Dalk.* V9
30 Telephone Ho. J15
19 Telfer Subway K15
22 Telferton Q17
10 Telford Coll. of Further Education K18
10 Telford Dr. J18
10 Telford Gdns. J18
10 Telford Pl. J18
10 Telford Rd. J17
31 Temple Park Cr. K15
16 Templeland Gro. F16
16 Templeland Rd. F16
12 Tennant St. N18
7 Teviot Pl. M16
34 Teviotbank Ho. R14
19 Teviotdale Pl. L17
37 Third Gait D12
32 Thirlestane La. M14

32 Thirlestane Rd. M15
Thistle Ct.*=Thistle St.
34 Thistle Foundation Homes Q14
19 Thistle Pl. L15
6 Thistle St. M17
6 Thistle St. La., N.E. M17
6 Thistle St. La., N.W. M17
6 Thistle St. La., S.E. M17
6 Thistle St. La., S.W. M17
30 Thomas Clouston Clinic K20
38 Thomson Cr. E11
38 Thomson Dr. E11
38 Thomson Gro. E11
38 Thomson Rd. E11
Thomson's Ct.*=Grassmarket
40 Thorburn Gro. J11
40 Thorburn Rd. H11
12 Thorntree St. O18
12 Thorntreeside O18
13 Thornville Terr. O18
50 Thornybank Ind. Est. V10
6 Thornybauk L15
45 Threipmuir Av. C8
45 Threipmuir Gdns. C8
45 Threipmuir Pl. C8
12 Timber Bush O19
12 Tinto Pl. N18
31 Tipperlinn Rd. L14
Tobago Pl.*=Morrison St.
51 Todhills R11
20 Tolbooth Museum N16
12 Tolbooth Wynd N19
19 Tollcross L15
6 Tollcross Sch. L15
39 Torduff Reservoir G10
39 Torduff Rd. H10
6 Torphichen Pl. L16
6 Torphichen St. L16
39 Torphin Hill Golf Course G10
39 Torphin Rd. G11
14 Torrance Pk. F17
50 Torsonce Rd., *Dalk.* T9
Toward Ct.*=Craigievar Wynd
12 Tower Pl. O19
12 Tower St. O19
12 Tower St. La. O19
23 Towerbank Sch. R17
12 Town Hall, Leith N19
22 Town Hall, Portobello R16
12 Trafalgar La. N19
12 Trafalgar St. N19
48 Traprain Pl. P8
48 Traprain Terr. P8
17 Traquair Park W. G15
6 Traverse Theatre M16
27 Trefoil Sch. C13
41 Trench Knowe L11
33 Tressilian Gdns. O13
11 Trinity Acad. M19
12 Trinity Acad./Telford Coll. Annexe M19
11 Trinity Ct. L19
11 Trinity Cr. L19
11 Trinity Gro. L19
11 Trinity Mains L30
Trinity Mains*=East Trinity Rd.
11 Trinity Rd. L19
12 Trinity Sch. (Primary) M19
7 Tron Sq. M16
40 Tryst Pk. K11
39 Turlies, The H12
Turnbull's Entry*=Potterrow
44 Turner Av. B10
44 Turner Pk. C10
15 Turnhouse Golf Course C16
15 Turnhouse Farm Rd. C17
15 Turnhouse Rd. D16
34 Tweedsmuir Ho. R14
29 Tyler's Acre Av. G15

29 Tyler's Acre Gdns. G15
29 Tyler's Acre Rd. G15
Tynecastle
Bdgs.*=McLeod St.
18 Tynecastle La. K15
18 Tynecastle Pk. (Hearts
F.C.) K15
Tynecastle Pl.*=Gorgie
Rd.
18 Tynecastle Sch. K15
30 Tynecastle Sch. Annexe
J15
Tynecastle Terr.*=Gorgie
Rd.

35 UCI Cinema S14
21 Ulster Cr. P16
21 Ulster Dr. P16
21 Ulster Gdns. P16
21 Ulster Gro. P16
21 Ulster Terr. P16
Union Ct*=Richmond Pl.
7 Union Pl. N17
7 Union St. N17
7 University Library M15
7 University of Edinburgh
M16
20 Upper Bow M16
49 Upper Broomieknowe R8
18 Upper Coltbridge Terr.
K16
34 Upper Craigour Q13
34 Upper Craigour Way P13
8 Upper Cramond Ct. E18
19 Upper Damside L16
19 Upper Dean Terr. L17
19 Upper Gilmore Pl. L15
19 Upper Gilmore Terr. L15
32 Upper Gray St. N15
6 Upper Grove Pl. L15
6 Usher Hall L16
32 Usher Institute M15

19 Valleyfield St. L15
12 Vanburgh Pl. O18
22 Vandeleur Av. Q17
22 Vandeleur Gro. Q17
22 Vandeleur Pl. Q17
19 Veitch's Sq. L17
6 Vennel M16
33 Ventnor Pl. O14
32 Ventnor Terr. N14
Vernon Cotts.*=Pittville
St. La.
35 Vexhim Pk. R15
16 Victor Park Terr. F16
12 Victoria Pk. M19
12 Victoria Sch. M20
7 Victoria St. M16
Victoria Terr.*=Victoria St.
25 Victoria Terr., Muss. W15
49 View Bk. S8
49 Viewbank Av. S9
49 Viewbank Cr. S8
49 Viewbank Dr. S8
49 Viewbank Rd. R8
49 Viewbank Vw. S8
29 Viewcraig Gdns. N16
20 Viewcraig St. N16
49 Viewfield S8
39 Viewfield Rd. G12
31 Viewforth L15
31 Viewforth Gdns. L15
31 Viewforth Sq. L15
31 Viewforth Terr. L15
49 Viewpark Gdns. R8
Violet Bk.*=Spring Gdns.
31 Violet Terr. K15
9 Vivian Terr. G18

12 Waddell Pl. N18
48 Wadingburn La. Q9
48 Wadingburn Rd. Q8
22 Wakefield Av. Q17
49 Walker Cr. S9

6 Walker St. L16
19 Walker Terr. L16
33 Walter Scott Av. O13
35 Wanton Walls T15
11 Wardie Av. L19
11 Wardie Cr. L19
11 Wardie Dell L19
11 Wardie Gro. K19
Wardie House
La.*=Boswall Rd.
11 Wardie Pk. L19
11 Wardie Rd. L19
11 Wardie Sch. L19
11 Wardie Sq. L19
11 Wardie Steps L19
11 Wardieburn Dr. K19
11 Wardieburn Pl. E. K30
10 Wardieburn Pl. N. K19
10 Wardieburn Pl. S. K19
10 Wardieburn Pl. W. K19
10 Wardieburn Rd. K19
10 Wardieburn St. E. K19
10 Wardieburn St. W. K19
10 Wardieburn Terr. K19
11 Wardiefield K19
30 Wardlaw Pl. K15
30 Wardlaw St. K15
30 Wardlaw Terr. K15
32 Warrender Park Cr. L15
32 Warrender Park Rd. M15
32 Warrender Park Terr. M15
36 Warriston C11
11 Warriston Av. M18
Warriston Cl.*=High St.
11 Warriston Cr. M18
11 Warriston Crem. M18
11 Warriston Dr. L18
11 Warriston Gdns. L18
11 Warriston Gro. L18
11 Warriston Pl. M18
11 Warriston Rd. M19
11 Warriston Terr. L18
19 Washington La. K15
19 Washington St. K15
12 Water St. O19
7 Waterloo Pl. M17
Waterside Ct.*=Coltbridge
Av.
Water's Cl.*=Shore
32 Watertoun Rd. N14
31 Watson Cr. K15
Watson's Bdgs.*=Main St.
24 Watts Cl., Muss. U15
34 Wauchope Av. Q14
34 Wauchope Cr. Q14
34 Wauchope Ho. Q14
34 Wauchope Pl. Q14
34 Wauchope Rd. Q14
34 Wauchope Sq. Q14
34 Wauchope Terr. Q14
49 Waugh Path S8
45 Waukmill La. D10
7 Waverley Bridge M16
49 Waverley Cr. S8
49 Waverley Dr. S8
7 Waverley Market M16
21 Waverley Pk. (Abbeyhill)
O17
49 Waverley Pk. (Bonnyrigg)
S8
21 Waverley Park Terr. O17
49 Waverley Rd. S8
50 Waverley Rd., Dalk. T9
21 Waverley Pl. O17
7 Waverley Sta. M16
7 Waverley Steps M16
49 Waverley Terr. S8
38 Weaver's Knowe Cr. D11
Websters Land*=West
Port
25 Wedderburn Ho., Muss.
V14
25 Wedderburn Terr., Muss.
V14
49 Wee Brae R9
50 Weir Cr. T9
29 Weir Ct. F13

19 Well Ct. L16
12 Wellington Pl. O19
7 Wellington St. N17
6 Wemyss Pl. L17
Wemyss Pl.
Mews*=Wemyss Pl.
20 West Adam St. N16
20 West Annandale St. M18
6 West Approach Rd. L16
6 West Bow M16
12 West Bowling Green St.
N19
22 West Brighton Cr. R16
10 West Broompark K20
31 West Bryson Rd. K15
41 West Caiystane Rd. L11
39 West Carnethy Av. H11
31 West Castle Rd. L15
18 West Catherine Pl. K16
18 West Coates Pl. K16
7 West College St. M16
18 West Ct., Ravelston J17
34 West Ct., Niddrie Q14
16 West Craigs D16
16 West Craigs Av. D15
16 West Craigs Cr. E15
16 West Craigs Gr. E15
26 West Croft A13
West Cromwell
St.*=Cromwell Pl.
20 West Crosscauseway N15
43 West Edge P10
6 West End L16
19 West End Pl. K15
11 West Ferryfield K18
19 West Fountain Pl. K15
30 West Gorgie Pk. J14
West Grange
Gdns.*=Grange Ln.
10 West Granton Cr. H19
10 West Granton Dr. J19
10 West Granton Gdns. J19
10 West Granton Gr. H19
10 West Granton Gro. J19
10 West Granton Ln. J19
10 West Granton Pl. H19
10 West Granton Rd. J30
10 West Granton Row J19
10 West Granton Terr. J19
10 West Granton Vw. J19
10 West Harbour Rd. K20
27 West Hermiston D13
24 West Holmes Gdns.,
Muss. U15
32 West Mains Rd. N13
19 West Maitland St. L16
32 West Mayfield N14
West Mill La.*=Dean Path
39 West Mill Rd. G11
32 West Newington Pl. N15
7 West Nicolson St. N16
7 West Norton Pl. N17
19 West Park Pl. K15
10 West Pier K20
10 West Pilton Av. J18
10 West Pilton Bk. H19
10 West Pilton Cr. H19
10 West Pilton Crossway J19
10 West Pilton Dr. J19
10 West Pilton Gdns. J19
10 West Pilton Gr. J19
10 West Pilton Gro. J19
10 West Pilton Lea J19
10 West Pilton Ln. J19
10 West Pilton Pk. (street) J19
10 West Pilton Pk. J18
10 West Pilton Pl. J19
10 West Pilton Rise J19
10 West Pilton Rd. J19
10 West Pilton St. J19
10 West Pilton Terr. J19
10 West Pilton Vw. J18
6 West Port M16
6 West Port House M16
32 West Preston St. N15
6 West Princes St. Gdns.
M16
6 West Register Ho. L16

7 West Register St. M17
32 West Relugas Rd. M14
7 West Richmond St. N16
32 West Savile Rd. N14
32 West Savile Terr. N14
10 West Shore Rd. H20
19 West Silvermills La. L17
47 West Straiton Cotts. O9
22 West Telferton Q17
6 West Tollcross L15
10 West Werberside K18
10 West Winnelstrae K18
10 West Woods K18
22 Westbank Ln. R17
22 Westbank Pl. R17
22 Westbank St. R17
38 Westburn Av. F12
38 Westburn Gdns. F12
38 Westburn Gro. F12
38 Westburn Middlefield F12
38 Westburn Park F12
28 Westburn Sch. F13
28 Wester Broom Av. F15
28 Wester Broom Dr. F15
28 Wester Broom Gdns. F15
28 Wester Broom Gro. F15
28 Wester Broom Pl. F15
28 Wester Broom Terr. F15
Wester Cl.*=Newhaven
Main St
18 Wester Coates Av. K16
18 Wester Coates Gdns. K16
18 Wester Coates Pl. K16
18 Wester Coates Rd. K16
18 Wester Coates Terr. K16
30 Wester Craiglockhart Hill
J13
10 Wester Drylaw Av. H18
10 Wester Drylaw Dr. H18
10 Wester Drylaw Pk. J18
10 Wester Drylaw Pl. H18
10 Wester Drylaw Row J17
38 Wester Hailes Centre F12
39 Wester Hailes Dr. F12
28 Wester Hailes Education
Centre F13
29 Wester Hailes Health
Centre F13
39 Wester Hailes Pk. G12
28 Wester Hailes Rd. F13
48 Wester Melville Q9
31 Wester Steil K13
18 Westerlea Sch. J16
Western
Corner*=Saughtonhall
Dr.
18 Western Gdns. J16
18 Western General Hosp.
K18
18 Western Pl. J16
18 Western Terr. J16
49 Westfield S9
30 Westfield Av. J15
30 Westfield Ct. J15
50 Westfield Gro. T9
50 Westfield Pk. T9
30 Westfield Rd. J15
30 Westfield St. J15
39 Westgarth Av. H11
31 Westhall Gdns. L15
Westland Cotts.*=
Ravenscroft Pl.
Westland Houses*=
Ravenscroft Pl.
49 Westmill Rd. R8
Westmost Cl.*=Newhaven
Main St.
30 Wheatfield Pl. J15
30 Wheatfield Rd. J15
30 Wheatfield St. K15
30 Wheatfield Terr. J15
50 Wheatsheaf La. U10
29 Whinhill Pk. G14
Whins Pl.*=Figgate St.
41 White Dales M11
41 White Ho. K10
30 White Pk. K15
30 White Pk. (Str.) K15

18 Whitehall Ct. **H17**
24 Whitehill Av., *Muss.* **U15**
50 Whitehill Dr., *Dalk.* **V9**
24 Whitehill Farm Rd., *Muss.*
U14
24 Whitehill Gdns., *Muss.*
U14
50 Whitehill Gr., *Dalk.* **V9**
35 Whitehill Mains **S14**
35 Whitehill Rd. **S14**
35 Whitehill St **S14**
7 Whitehorse Cl. **N16**
31 Whitehouse Ln. **L15**
8 Whitehouse Rd. **E18**
32 Whitehouse Terr. **M14**
38 Whitelaw **E12**
44 Whitelea Cr. **C8**
44 Whitelea Rd. **B8**
Whites Cl.*=St. Andrew
St.
12 Whitingford **M19**
30 Whitson Cr. **H15**
30 Whitson Gro. **H15**
30 Whitson Pl. E. **H15**
30 Whitson Pl. W. **H15**
30 Whitson Rd. **H15**
30 Whitson Terr. **H15**
30 Whitson Walk **H15**
30 Whitson Way **H15**
21 Whyte Pl. **O17**
21 Wilfred Terr. **P17**
William Jameson
Pl.*=Pipe St.
William Jamieson
St.*=Pipe St.
6 William St. **L16**
6 William St. La., N.E. **L16**
6 William St. La., N.W. **L16**
6 William St. La., S.E. **L16**
6 William St. La., S.W. **L16**
Williamfield*=Rosefield
Av.
Williamfield
Sq.*=Rosefield Av.
12 Willowbank Row **M19**
21 Willowbrae Av. **P16**
21 Willowbrae Gdns. **P16**
21 Willowbrae Rd. **P16**
30 Willowpark Sch. **J15**
50 Wilson Av., *Dalk.* **V10**
23 Wilson's Pk. **R17**
32 Wilton Rd. **N13**
Windmill La*=Buccleuch
Pl.
Windmill Pl.*=Chapel St.
25 Windsor Gdns., *Muss.*
W15
25 Windsor Pk., *Muss.* **W15**
25 Windsor Park Dr., *Muss.*
W15
25 Windsor Park Pl., *Muss.*
W15
25 Windsor Park Terr., *Muss.*
W15
23 Windsor Pl. **R16**
20 Windsor St. **N17**
20 Windsor St. La. **N17**
25 Windy Wynd, *Muss.* **V14**
41 Winton Dr. **M10**
41 Winton Gdns. **M10**
41 Winton Gro. **L11**
41 Winton Ln. **M10**
41 Winton Pk. **L10**
41 Winton Terr. **L10**
49 Wishart Av. **S8**
49 Wishart Pl. **T9**
21 Wishaw Terr. **O17**
34 Wisp Gr. **R14**
35 Wisp, The **R14**
42 Wolrige Rd. **O12**
21 Wolseley Cr. **P17**
Wolseley
Gdns.*=Wolseley Cr.
Wolseley Pl.*=Wolseley
Cr.
21 Wolseley Terr. **P17**
31 Wood Pl. **L14**
13 Woodbine Terr. **O18**

50 Woodburn Av., *Dalk.* **V10**
50 Woodburn Bk., *Dalk.* **V10**
50 Woodburn Dr., *Dalk.* **U10**
50 Woodburn Gdns., *Dalk.*
V10
50 Woodburn Gr., *Dalk.* **V9**
31 Woodburn Ho. **M14**
50 Woodburn Ln., *Dalk.* **V10**
50 Woodburn Medway, *Dalk.*
V10
50 Woodburn Pk., *Dalk.* **V10**
50 Woodburn Pl., *Dalk.* **V9**
Woodburn Pl.*=Canaan
La.
50 Woodburn Rd., *Dalk.* **U10**
50 Woodburn Sch., *Dalk.*
V10
50 Woodburn St., *Dalk.* **V10**
31 Woodburn Terr. **L14**
50 Woodburn Terr., *Dalk.* **V9**
50 Woodburn Vw., *Dalk.* **V9**
39 Woodfield Av. **G11**
39 Woodfield Pk. **G11**
39 Woodhall Av. **F11**
39 Woodhall Bk. **G11**
38 Woodhall Dr. **F11**
39 Woodhall Gro. **G11**
39 Woodhall Mains **F11**
39 Woodhall Millbrae **G11**
39 Woodhall Rd. **G11**
38 Woodhall Terr. **F11**
22 Woodlands Gro. **Q15**
25 Woodside Gdns., *Muss.*
W15
23 Woodside Terr. **S16**
33 Woodstock Pl. **O13**
13 Woodville Terr. **O18**
51 Woolmet Cr. **R12**
20 Wright's Houses **L15**
32 Wyvern Pk. **M14**

12 Yardheads **N19**
19 Yeaman La. **L15**
19 Yeaman Pl. **K15**
42 Yewlands Cr. **O12**
42 Yewlands Gdns. **O12**
Yoole Pl.*=Pipe St.
York Bdgs.*=Queen St.
7 York La. **M17**
7 York Pl. **M17**
11 York Rd. **M19**
6 Young St. **L16**
6 Young St. La., N. **L16**
6 Young St. La., S. **L16**

11 Zetland Pl. **L19**
17 Zoo **G16**